4th

Science
Daily Practice Workbook
20 weeks of fun activities

ARGOPREP

Physical Science • **Life Science** • **Earth & Space Science** • **Engineering**

ArgoPrep is one of the leading providers of supplemental educational products and services. We offer affordable and effective test prep solutions to educators, parents and students. Learning should be fun and easy! To access more resources visit us at www.argoprep.com.

Our goal is to make your life easier, so let us know how we can help you by e-mailing us at: info@argoprep.com.

- ArgoPrep is a recipient of the prestigious **Mom's Choice Award**.

- ArgoPrep also received the 2019 **Seal of Approval** from Homeschool.com for our award-winning workbooks.

- ArgoPrep was awarded the 2019 **National Parenting Products Award**, **Gold Medal Parent's Choice Award** and **the Tillywig Brain Child Award**.

SCIENCE SERIES

Science Daily Practice Workbook by ArgoPrep is an award-winning series created by certified science teachers to help build mastery of foundational science skills. Our workbooks explore science topics in depth with ArgoPrep's 5 E'S to build science mastery: Engaging, Exploring, Explaining, Experimenting, and Elaborating. All of our curriculum is aligned with the latest Next Generation Science Standards.

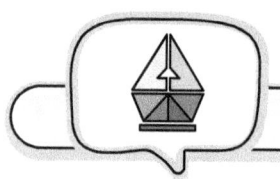
Introduction

Welcome to your Grade 4 Science Workbook! In this workbook you will spend one week per a topic exploring such incredible fields of science including biology, Earth and space science, physical science and engineering. You will start with physical science and learn about energy and the many forms it comes in. After that you will move on to biology where we will discuss plants and animals, how organisms sense the world around them and more! Next comes Earth and Space sciences where we will talk about the processes that change Earth and how humans impact the resources on our planet. Lastly we will focus on engineering and learn how to solve problems using science and creativity!

As always, feel free to dive into these topics more using resources like the Internet, especially if you are passionate about a topic. Go at your own pace and use the Answer Key when you get stuck on a problem. And as always, remember that you are a scientist and can learn so much about the world around you each and every day!

Table of Contents

How to Use the Book

All 20 weeks of daily activity pages in this book follow the same weekly structure. The book is divided into four sections: Physical Science, Life Science, Earth & Space Science and Engineering. The activities in each of the sections align to the Next Generation Science Standards which will help prepare students for state standardized assessments. While the sections can be completed in any order, it is important to complete each week within the section in chronological order, as the skills often build upon one another. Each week focuses on one specific topic within the section. More information about the weekly structure can be found in the Weekly Planner section.

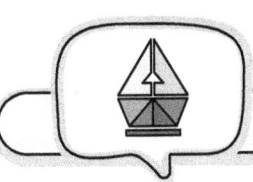
Weekly Planner

Day	Activity	Description
1	Engaging with the Topic	Read a short text on the topic and answer multiple choice questions.
2	Exploring the Topic	Interact with the topic on a deeper level by collecting, analyzing and interpreting data.
3	Explaining the Topic	Make sense of the topic by explaining and beginning to draw conclusions about the data.
4	Experimenting with the Topic	Investigate the topic through hands-on, easy to implement experiments.
5	Elaborating on the Topic	Reflect on the topic and use all information learned to draw conclusions and evaluate results.

How to access video explanations?

Go to **argoprep.com/science4**
OR scan the QR Code:

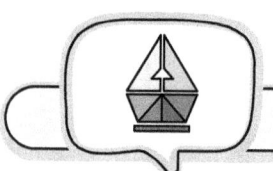

List of Topics

Unit	Week	Topic	Standard
Physical Science	1	Speed & Energy	4-PS3-1
Physical Science	2	Energy Transfer	4-PS3-2
Physical Science	3	Changes In Speed & Energy	4-PS3-3
Physical Science	4	Energy Conversion	4-PS3-4
Physical Science	5	Modeling Waves	4-PS4-1
Physical Science	6	Perception Of Light	4-PS4-2
Physical Science	7	Information Transfer	4-PS4-3
Life Science	8	Animal Structures & Their Functions	4-LS1-1
Life Science	9	Plant Structures & Their Functions	4-LS1-1
Life Science	10	The Senses	4-LS1-2
Life Science	11	Responding To Stimuli	4-LS1-2
Earth & Space Science	12	Earth's Changes Over Time	4-ESS1-1
Earth & Space Science	13	Weathering & Erosion	4-ESS2-1
Earth & Space Science	14	Earth's Physical Features	4-ESS2-2
Earth & Space Science	15	Renewable & Nonrenewable Energy	4-ESS3-1
Earth & Space Science	16	Human Impact On Earth	4-ESS3-2
Engineering	17	Defining Design Problems	3-5-ETS1-1
Engineering	18	Design Constraints	3-5-ETS1-1
Engineering	19	Comparing Solutions	3-5-ETS1-2
Engineering	20	Improving Ideas & Designs	3-5-ETS1-3

Next Generation Science Standards Correlation Guide

Unit	Week	Next Generation Science Standard	Description of Standard
Physical Science	1	4-PS3-1	Use evidence to construct an explanation relating the speed of an object to the energy of that object.
Physical Science	2	4-PS3-2	Make observations to provide evidence that energy can be transferred from place to place by sound, light, heat, and electric currents.
Physical Science	3	4-PS3-3	Ask questions and predict outcomes about the changes in energy that occur when objects collide.
Physical Science	4	4-PS3-4	Apply scientific ideas to design, test, and refine a device that converts energy from one form to another.
Physical Science	5	4-PS4-1	Develop a model of waves to describe patterns in terms of amplitude and wavelength and that waves can cause objects to move.
Physical Science	6	4-PS4-2	Develop a model to describe that light reflecting from objects and entering the eye allows objects to be seen
Physical Science	7	4-PS4-3	Generate and compare multiple solutions that use patterns to transfer information.
Life Science	8	4-LS1-1	Construct an argument that animals have internal and external structures that function to support survival, growth, behavior, and reproduction.

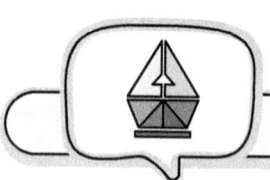
Unit	Week	Next Generation Science Standard	Description of Standard
Life Science	9	4-LS1-1	Construct an argument that plants have internal and external structures that function to support survival, growth, behavior, and reproduction.
Life Science	10	4-LS1-2	Use a model to describe that animals receive different types of information through their senses and process the information in their brain.
Life Science	11	4-LS1-2	Use a model to describe how animals process information in their brain and respond to the information in different ways.
Earth & Space Science	12	4-ESS1-1	Identify evidence from patterns in rock formations and fossils in rock layers to support an explanation for changes in a landscape over time.
Earth & Space Science	13	4-ESS2-1	Make observations and/or measurements to provide evidence of the effects of weathering or the rate of erosion by water, ice, wind, or vegetation.
Earth & Space Science	14	4-ESS2-2	Analyze and interpret data from maps to describe patterns of Earth's features.
Earth & Space Science	15	4-ESS3-1	Obtain and combine information to describe that energy and fuels are derived from natural resources and their uses affect the environment.
Earth & Space Science	16	4-ESS3-2	Generate and compare multiple solutions to reduce the impacts of natural Earth processes on humans.

Unit	Week	Next Generation Science Standard	Description of Standard
Engineering	17	3-5-ETS1-1	Define a simple design problem reflecting a need or a want.
Engineering	18	3-5-ETS1-1	Define a simple design problem reflecting a need or a want that includes specified criteria for success and constraints on materials, time, or cost.
Engineering	19	3-5-ETS1-2	Generate and compare multiple possible solutions to a problem based on how well each is likely to meet the criteria and constraints of the problem.
Engineering	20	3-5-ETS1-3	Plan and carry out fair tests in which variables are controlled and failure points are considered to identify aspects of a model or prototype that can be improved.

WEEK 1

Physical Science

Speed & Energy

4-PS3-1

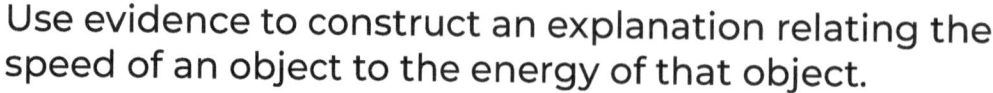

Use evidence to construct an explanation relating the speed of an object to the energy of that object.

ARGOPREP

Directions: Read the text below. Then answer the questions that follow.

Speed Is A Measure Of Energy

Energy is something that we encounter and use every day. If you have a lot of energy, it means you can do a lot of activities. In science, energy is the ability to do work or to move an object. Today, you are going to focus on the energy of movement which is known as **kinetic energy**.

When something is moving very fast, it has a lot of energy. Think about a race car speeding around a track - it takes a lot of energy in order to make the car go that quickly. Now think about if that car slowed down enough so that you could walk alongside of it. The car is using much less energy. **Speed** is a way for us to measure energy. If something is moving very fast, it has a lot of energy. If something is moving slow, it has less energy.

1. Energy is defined as:

   A. A bunch of sugar

   B. A speeding car

   C. The ability to do work

   D. When an object is not moving

2. Energy in the form of movement is known as what?

   A. Kinetic energy

   B. Sugar energy

   C. Gasoline energy

   D. Fast energy

3. If something is moving slowly, how much energy does it have?

   A. A lot of energy

   B. A little bit of energy

   C. No energy at all

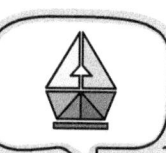
Yesterday, you learned about the relationship between speed and kinetic energy. Today you will explore this relationship through a few activities.

Directions: Read each text below and complete the activity. Then answer the questions that follow.

Exercise & Energy

Find a space where you can run around easily, such as the park or an athletic field. If running is not something you can do, try another type of exercise that uses just your arms. Set a timer and walk for 2 minutes. At the end of 2 minutes, notice how you feel. Set the timer again for 2 minutes and run at a very quick pace. At the end of 2 minutes, notice how you feel.

1. Were you more tired after walking for two minutes or after running for two minutes?

 A. Walking

 B. Running

Wind Energy

Take a ping-pong ball and place it on a flat surface. Place your face right next to it and blow on it lightly. Notice how far it rolls. Now place the ping-pong ball back in the same spot and blow on it as hard as you can. Notice how far it rolls this time.

2. Did the ping-pong ball roll further when you blew on it lightly or as hard as you could?

 A. Blow lightly

 B. Blow hard

3. Did the ping-pong ball roll faster when you blew on it lightly or as hard as you could?

 A. Blow lightly

 B. Blow hard

Speedy Sliding

Sit at the top of a slide and then slide down it. Now, have a friend or a parent push you at the top of the slide. Feel free to slide a few times both with and without a push.

4. Did you travel down the slide faster when you slide on your own or when you got a push from a friend?

    A. On your own

    B. With a push

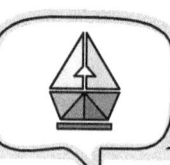
Yesterday, you explored how energy and speed are related with some activities and demos. Today you will explain how this relationship works.

Directions: Read each text below. Then answer the questions that follow.

Exercise & Energy

You discovered that you are more tired after running than after walking for the same amount of time.

1. Why do you feel tired after running? Think about how movement relates to energy.

....

....

....

....

Wind Energy

You discovered that a ping-pong ball will roll further and faster if you blow on it forcefully than if you blow on it lightly.

2. Where did the ping-pong ball get its energy from in order for it to be able to move?

....

....

....

Speedy Sliding

You discovered that you slide down a slide faster when you get a push from a friend.

3. Why do you think getting a push from a friend makes you slide down a slide faster?

....

....

....

You have spent several days learning about, exploring and explaining how speed and energy are related. Today you will experiment how speed and energy relate to a marble being used to knock over dominos.

Materials:

1. Marble
2. Blocks or legos
3. Cardboard
4. Tape
5. A meter stick

Procedure:

1. Start by making three different ramps with your blocks or legos. Make the ramps three different heights so that you have a short, a medium and a tall ramp. In order to make the ramp smooth for the marble ro roll down, you can lay a piece of cardboard over the top of the blocks or legos so that it is a flat, even hill. You may need to tape it in place.

2. Place the ramps on flat ground and make sure there is nothing around it.

3. Take your marble and place it at the top of the short ramp. Let it go so that it rolls down the ramp. Notice how quickly it travels and record your observations in the table on the next page. Measure the distance the marble rolled away from the bottom of the ramp and record it in the table below.

4. Repeat step #3 with your medium and your tall ramps.

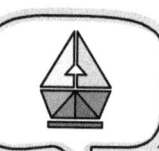
Data Table:

	Short Ramp	Medium Ramp	Tall Ramp
Speed Of The Marble (fast vs. slow)			
Distance Marble Rolled in inches			

Follow Up Questions:

1. Which ramp made the marble roll fastest?

....

....

2. Which ramp made the marble roll furthest?

....

....

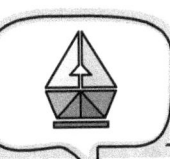
Yesterday, you created three different ramps and observed how they changed the movement of a marble. Today you will elaborate on your findings.

Directions: Read and answer each question below.

1. A marble that has more energy will roll ....

   A. Faster

   B. Further

   C. Slower

   D. Both A & B are correct

2. Which ramp caused the marble to have more energy?

   A. Short ramp

   B. Medium ramp

   C. Tall ramp

3. If you wanted to make your marble roll even faster, what could you do?

   ....

   ....

   ....

   ....

4. Can you think of another way to show that things that move faster have more energy?

Physical Science

Energy Transfer

4-PS3-2

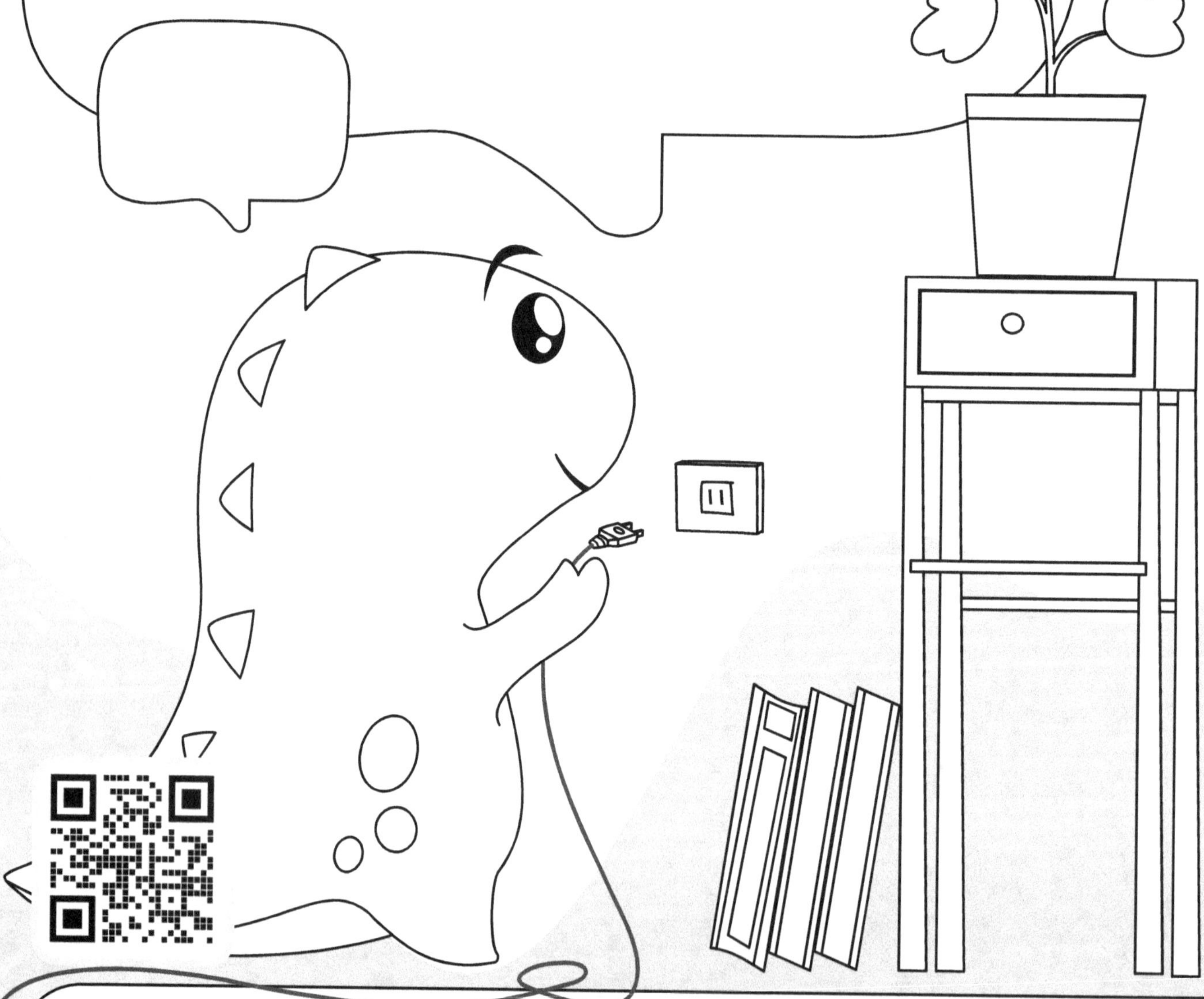

Make observations to provide evidence that energy can be transferred from place to place by sound, light, heat, and electric currents.

Directions: Read the text below. Then answer the questions that follow.

Energy Can Move From Place To Place

Energy comes in lots of different forms including electricity, heat, sounds and light. **Electricity** is transported through wires around our towns and cities so that it can be used to power businesses and many things in our home. **Heat** can be generated to keep temperatures warm in buildings when it is cold outside. A loud **sound** can travel really far distances, so far that sometimes you cannot even see the place where the sound came from. The sun's **light** travels more than 94 million miles to get to Earth. In conclusion, energy can be transferred or moved from one place to another.

1. Which of the following is not a type of energy?

   A. Sound

   B. Light

   C. Electricity

   D. Metal

2. What type of energy is used to keep your house warm in the winter?

   A. Sound

   B. Electricity

   C. Heat

   D. Light

3. True or false? Energy can be transferred from one place to another.

   A. True

   B. False

Yesterday, you learned that energy can move or be moved from one place to another place. Today you will explore this idea through some activities and observations.

Directions: Read each text below and complete the activity. Then answer the questions that follow.

Can You Hear It?

Turn on a radio or a television so that the volume is medium to loud. Walk out of the room so that you can no longer see the radio or the television but you can still hear it. You can adjust the volume to be louder if you need to.

1. Were you able to hear the sound even if you walked away from the source of the sound?

A. Yes   **B.** No

Warm & Cozy

This works best is you are wearing a black or dark colored shirt since dark colors absorb heat and light energy. Stand in front of a window on a bright and sunny day with your back towards the sunlight. Stand there for a few minutes and notice how the temperature of your back changes or feels.

2. How did the temperature change when you stood in the light for a few minutes?

....

....

3. The sun coming in from the window has what two types of energy?
  A. Light
  B. Sound
  C. Heat

Traveling Current

Go around your house and identify where you see electrical sockets in the wall. Notice if there are cords plugged into them and what types of appliances those cords lead to.

4. What is the job of an electrical cord of an appliance when it is plugged into an electrical socket?

   A. Hold an appliance in place

   B. Bring electricity from the electrical socket to the appliance

   C. Stop an appliance from working or turning on

Yesterday, you explored different ways that energy can travel from place to place. Today you will explain how this works or how you experienced it yesterday.

Directions: Read each text below. Then answer the questions that follow.

Can You Hear It?

You discovered that you can hear sound even if you cannot see where the sound comes from so long as the sound is loud enough.

1. Where did the sound start and where did the sound end in this activity?

Warm & Cozy

You discovered that your back begins to feel warm when you stand in sunlight for a while.

2. Where does the energy from the light coming in through the window come from?

3. Is heat a type of energy that can travel from place to place?

    A. Yes

    B. No

Traveling Current

You discovered that electrical cords helps electricity travel from an electrical socket to an appliance that needs electricity in order to work.

4. If you only had one electrical socket in your home, and you needed to power a television on the other side of your home, what would you need?

You have spent several days exploring and explaining how energy can travel from place to place. Today you will experiment with this concept.

Materials:

1. 3 identical mason jars with lids
2. Water
3. Thermometer

Procedure:

1. Start by filling each mason jar completely with room temperature water. Take the temperature of the water and record it in the table below.

2. Screw a lid onto each jar.

3. Place one jar in a cabinet or closet that is completely dark. Place the second jar in front of a window that has sun coming in through it. Place the last jar in a room that only has electrical lights on but no sunlight - if there are windows in this room you can just close the blinds or make sure the jar is nowhere near the window.

4. Leave the jars alone for a few hours. Then open each jar and measure its temperature with the thermometer. Record your data in the table on the next page.

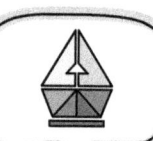

Data Table:

	Jar In Closet/ Cabinet	Jar In Sunlight	Jar In Room With Electric Lights
Beginning Temperature of Water			
End Temperature of Water			

Follow Up Questions:

1. Which jar had the warmest temperature by the end of the experiment?

....

....

2. Which jar had the coldest temperature by the end of the experiment?

....

....

Yesterday, you experimented with how light can change the temperature of water in a jar. Today you will elaborate on what you learned from this experiment.

Directions: Read and answer each question below.

1. What type of energy is temperature a measure of?

   A. Electricity

   B. Sound

   C. Heat

2. Why do you think the jar in the sunlight was warmer than the jar in the closet/ cabinet?

   _____

   _____

   _____

   _____

3. Do you think this experiment would have the same results if you did it at night? Why or why not?

   _____

   _____

   _____

   _____

4. If you were outside on a hot, sunny day, why would standing in the shade of a tree help cool you off?

   _____

   _____

   _____

   _____

Physical Science

Changes In Speed & Energy

4-PS3-3

Ask questions and predict outcomes about the changes in energy that occur when objects collide.

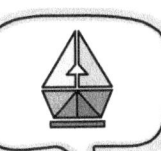
Directions: Read the text below. Then answer the questions that follow.

When Objects Collide

Over the past couple of weeks you have learned about different types of energy and how they can move from place to place. Today you will learn what happens when objects **collide**. When two objects come into contact with one another, or collide, movement is involved. Maybe you've heard of a car collision - this happens when a car hits another car or another object by accident. When one thing hits another thing, the energy they have have also changes. This week you will explore how energy changes by exploring different examples of collisions.

1. When two objects come into contact with each other, what is this called?

   A. Energy

   B. Collision

   C. Change

   D. Sound

2. True or false? The energy of objects changes when a collision occurs.

   A. True

   B. False

3. Which of these is an example of a collision?

   A. When a hammer hits a nail

   B. When you you get a high five from a friend

   C. When you strike a ball with a baseball bat

   D. All of the above

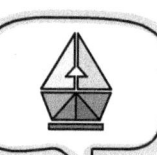
Yesterday, you learned that energy changes when two or more objects collide. Today you will explore this by completing activities with objects around your home.

Directions: Read each text below and complete the activity. Then answer the questions that follow.

Tennis Ball: Part 1

Take a tennis ball and sit on the ground in front of a wall. Roll the ball quickly towards the wall and watch what happens when the ball makes contact with the wall and how it moves after.

1. How did the ball's energy change after it made contact with the wall?

   A. It sped up

   B. It slowed down

2. When the ball hits the wall, what is this called?

   A. Energy

   B. Force

   C. Collision

Tennis Balls: Part 2

Take two tennis balls and place one of them about 2 feet in front of you. Roll the other tennis ball at the tennis ball in front of you, making sure they collide. If you miss a few times, just try again. Notice any movement that occurs when the two tennis balls collide.

3. What happened to the ball that was not moving when you hit it with the tennis ball that you rolled towards it?

....

....

....

The Domino Effect

Find a handful of dominos (5-8 dominoes) and line them up so they are about 1 an inch apart and standing up on their narrow end. Push the first domino down and observe what happens to the dominos lined up after it.

4. What happened to the dominos behind the first domino when you pushed only the first domino down with your finger?

....

....

....

....

....

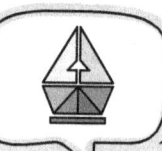
Yesterday, you explored different ways that energy can change when objects collide. Today you will explain what you observed.

Directions: Read each text below. Then answer the questions that follow.

Tennis Ball: Part 1

You discovered that when a tennis ball collides with a wall that it will slow down and change direction.

1. Did the wall move at all when the ball collided with it?

    A. Yes

    B. No

2. Did the tennis ball or the wall's energy look like it changed more because of the collision?

    A. The tennis ball's energy looked like it changed more

    B. The wall's energy looked like it changed more

Tennis Balls: Part 2

You discovered that when you roll a tennis ball towards another tennis ball that is sitting in one place, they will collide and both balls will move.

3. Did the ball you rolled speed up or slow down when it collided with the other tennis ball?

    A. Slowed down

    B. Sped up

4. In previous lessons you learned that movement is a form of energy known as kinetic energy. When an object speeds up or slows down, do you see that it is a change in the kinetic energy?

    A. Yes

    B. No

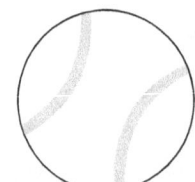

The Domino Effect

You discovered that when you push on one domino, the dominos lined up after it will fall down one at a time as a result.

5. Where did the energy come from that caused all of the dominos to fall down?

    A. A gust of wind

    B. The sun

    C. Your finger

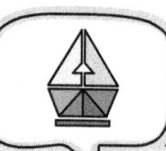
You have spent several days exploring and explaining how energy changes when objects collide with each other. Today you will experiment further with this idea.

Materials:

1. A piece of cardboard or poster board that is at least 3 feet by 3 feet
2. A handful of marbles of different sizes and colors
3. A ruler
4. A marker and a pencil
5. A piece of string that is 12 inches long or so

Procedure:

1. Mark a dot in the center of your poster board. Tie your pencil to one end of the string and hold the other end of the string on the dot in the center of your board. Make sure the string is taut and draw a circle with the marker, holding the string at the center dot the whole time.

2. Place a few marbles of different sizes and colors inside the circle. Choose one small marble to be the one you shoot at other marbles. You can look up videos of how to "shoot marbles" or you can just roll them if that is easier.

3. Try knocking all of the marbles out of the boundaries of the circle by shooting your chosen small marble at them. You can use your pencil to trace the pathway of marbles as they exit the circle. Some marbles might require multiple collisions in order to be knocked out of the circle.

4. Once all of the marbles are out, complete step #3 again, this time using your biggest marble as the marble you use to shoot the others out of the circle. Again observe how the marbles move, what directions they move, and how many collisions it takes for them to be knocked out of the circle.

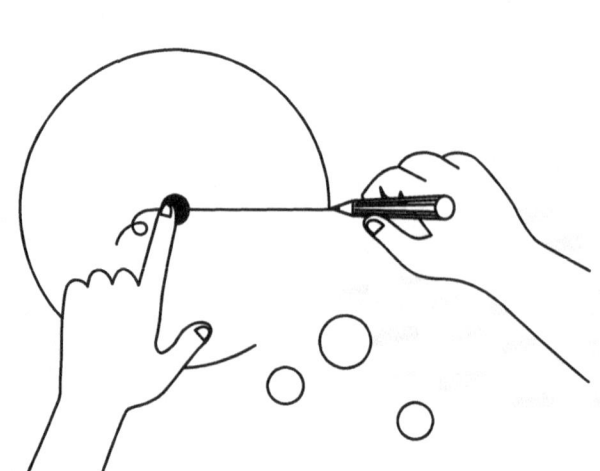

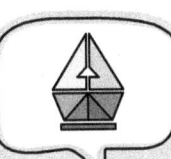
Follow-Up Questions:

1. Draw a diagram of what it looks like when two marbles collide. Use arrows to show what directions they move after they collide.

2. What marbles were easiest to knock out of the circle?

....

3. Do marbles get faster or slower the further they roll?

....

....

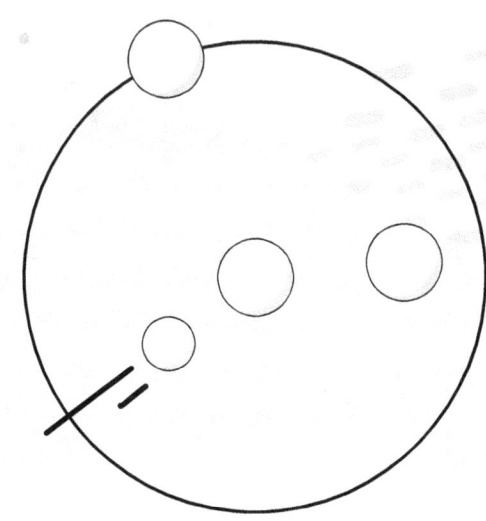

Yesterday, you experimented with marbles' energy changes when they collided with each other. Today you will elaborate on your findings.

Directions: Read and answer each question below.

1. When one marble hits another marble, what happens?

_____

_____

_____

2. If a marble is moving quickly, it has _____ energy than a marble that is not moving at all.

    A. More

    B. Less

    C. The same amount

3. If two things are moving slow and collide, will they move more or less than if two marbles are moving quick and collide?

_____

_____

_____

4. How did large marbles move differently than small marbles when they collided with another object?

_____

_____

_____

_____

_____

WEEK 4

Physical Science

Energy Conversion

4-PS3-4

Apply scientific ideas to design, test, and refine a device that converts energy from one form to another.

ARGOPREP

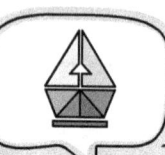
Directions: Read the text below. Then answer the questions that follow.

How Energy Is Converted

Pretend you are walking along the sidewalk on a warm, sunny spring day in the afternoon. The air is pleasant around you but when you put your hand on the asphalt, you notice it is much warmer, even hot to touch. Why is that? This has to do with the idea that energy can **convert** from one form of energy to another form of energy. The light energy from the sun is captured by the black asphalt and converted into heat energy. Another example of energy conversion happens when you eat food - the energy in food is converted into the energy of the movement you are doing when you are walking, talking or anything else!

1. Fill in the blank: energy can .... from one form of energy to another form of energy.

    A. Explode   **C.** Heat

    B. Convert   **D.** Jump

2. In the example in the reading, light energy from the sun is converted into what type of energy that you can feel coming from the asphalt?

    A. Heat   **C.** Movement

    B. Light   **D.** Food

3. What do you need to do in order to get more energy to do things like play sports and move around?

    A. Run faster

    B. Find a battery

    C. Sit still

    D. Eat

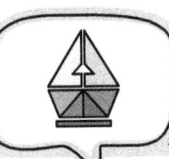
Yesterday, you learned that energy can change from one form to another. Today you will explore this idea through observations and activities.

Directions: Read each text below and complete the activity. Then answer the questions that follow.

Powering A Car

Take a moment to consider something that gas-powered cars need - fuel! The fuel is broken down by the engine of the car so that the car can be driven to wherever you want to go.

1. Gas in a car must contain which of the following?

A. Heat

B. Food

C. Light

D. Energy

Flashlight Conversion

Take a flashlight and unscrew the bottom of it. Notice how it contains one or more batteries. Batteries contain energy that is converted to electricity. Close the flashlight with the batteries in it and switch it on. You'll know it's on because a bright light will come out one end.

2. What type of energy was the electricity in the batteries converted into?

A. Heat

B. Movement

C. Light

D. Thermal

Cooking With Energy

When you turn on an oven, it gets really hot. Some ovens use electrical energy while others use energy from burning gas. The oven is then used to bake delicious food.

3. What type of energy is electricity or gas converted into when you turn on a stove?

A. Heat

B. Food

C. Light

D. Energy

Yesterday, you explored different ways that energy can be converted from one type to another. Today you will explain what you learned.

Directions: Read each text below. Then answer the questions that follow.

Powering A Car

You discovered that gas-powered cars run on the energy from fuel.

1. What type of energy does the car's engine convert fuel into?

    A. Light

    B. Chemical

    C. Movement

2. What happens when a car runs out of gas?

    ....

    ....

    ....

    ....

Flashlight Conversion

You discovered that flashlights convert battery electricity into light.

3. When you place your hand over the end of the flashlight that is giving off light, what other type of energy do you notice? Hint: you can feel this type of energy.

    ....

    ....

    ....

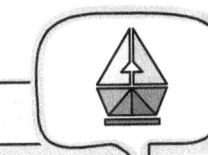

Cooking With Energy

You discovered that ovens can make heat out of either electricity or gas.

4. Do you see that the food in the oven needs heat energy in order to be baked or cooked?

   A. Yes

   B. No

5. What is one other thing in your home (or a friend's home) that converts either electricity or gas to heat?

....

....

....

....

You have spent several days exploring and explaining how energy can be converted from one form to another. Today you will experiment with the concept by creating a solar oven.

Background:

Solar power is power that is made by capturing the energy from the sun. The sun's light can be converted into solar power and solar heat. Today you are going to try to harness the heat from the sun and make a solar oven out of household items.

Materials:

1. A old pizza box (or something similar in shape and size)
2. Aluminum foil
3. Black construction paper
4. Scissors
5. Tape
6. Plastic wrap or a clear plastic ziplock bag
7. Newspapers
8. Ruler
9. Thermometer
10. Metal or foil pie pan

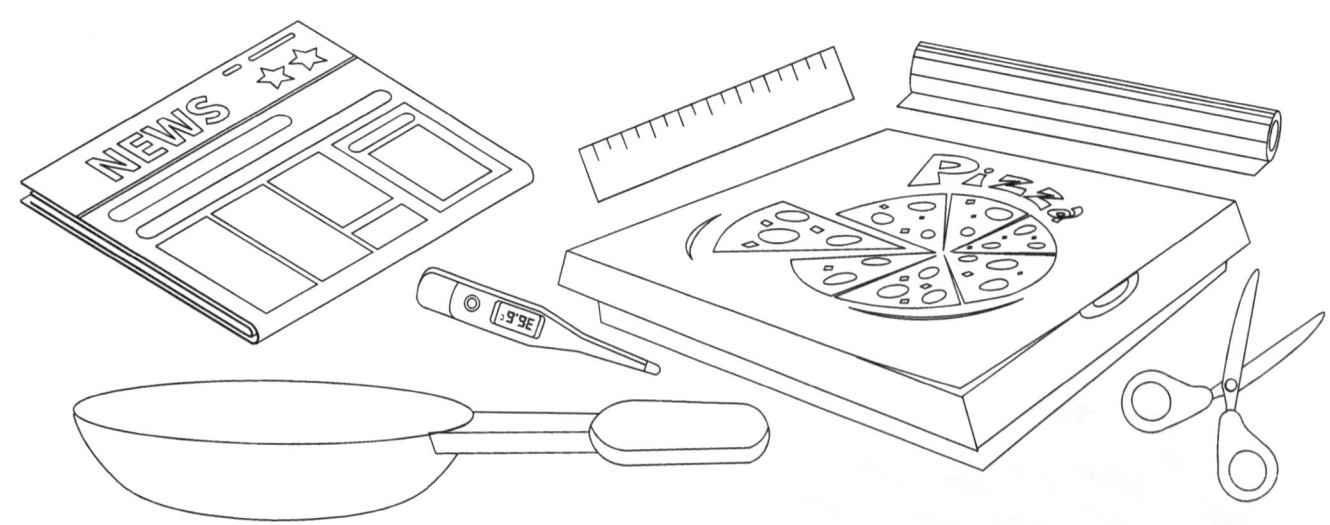

Procedure:

1. Trace a square on the top of the box so that one side touches the hinge of the box and the other three sides leave about a 2 inch space around the edge of the box. Cut those three sides, leaving the hinge side of the square uncut. This will make it so the square is still attached and you now have a flap.

2. Cover the square flap completely with a layer of aluminum foil.

3. Cover the top of the box (where space that the square was cut out of is) completely with a layer of clear plastic wrap and tape it down. You should still be able to open the pizza box as you normally would so that you can place something inside of it to cook.

4. Cover the bottom of the box with black paper - this helps to absorb heat in the same way that black asphalt absorbs heat from the sun due to the dark color.

5. Roll up three pieces of newspaper and place them inside the pizza box along with 4 edges - this is to help insulate your solar oven.

6. Place the pie pan inside the box and close it. Bring the oven outside on a sunny day and prop the aluminum flap open with a ruler so that it faces and catches the sun's light. You can alter the angle of your flap by moving the ruler so that more sun is directed inside the box.

7. Allow your own to "preheat" for about an hour or two and then place an egg inside the pan and close the oven. Time how long it takes for the egg to cook. You might have to move your oven to face the sun as the sun moves across the sky throughout the day. It will likely take longer for the egg to cook than if you were doing it on the stovetop.

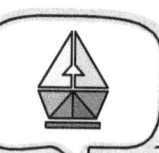
Yesterday, you experimented with energy conversion by building a solar oven. Today you will elaborate on how this process went and what you learned.

Directions: Read and answer each question below.

1. The sun's energy was converted into what type of energy in your solar oven?

    A. Heat

    B. Light

    C. Electric

2. Why did you need to cover the flap of the oven with aluminum foil?

3. Why did you need to line the inside of the oven with black paper?

4. Were you able to cook your egg?

5. Can your solar oven get as hot as the oven in your kitchen?

    A. Yes

    B. No

6. Can the sun's energy be converted into different forms of energy?

    A. Yes

    B. No

Physical Science

Modeling Waves

4-PS4-1

Develop a model of waves to describe patterns in terms of amplitude and wavelength and that waves can cause objects to move.

ARGOPREP

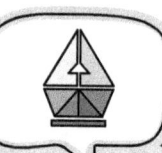
Directions: Read the text below. Then answer the questions that follow.

Waves Of Energy

Think about the shape of **waves** for a moment - you can even draw a few in spaces on this page! Notice how they move up and down. If you drew a few, they all probably looked very similar. Waves can be found in more places than the ocean. You can cook food with <u>microwaves</u>. You can look inside the body with <u>x-ray</u> waves, and you can get a sun tan (or a sunburn unfortunately) due to <u>light</u> waves. The <u>sounds</u> you hear are a type of wave. In physical science, waves are different ways that energy can travel. The speed of the wave is determined by the frequency of the wavelength or how often the wavelength repeats itself. The speed of waves is called wavelength. Look at the diagram below to see what the **wavelength** is of different types of waves.

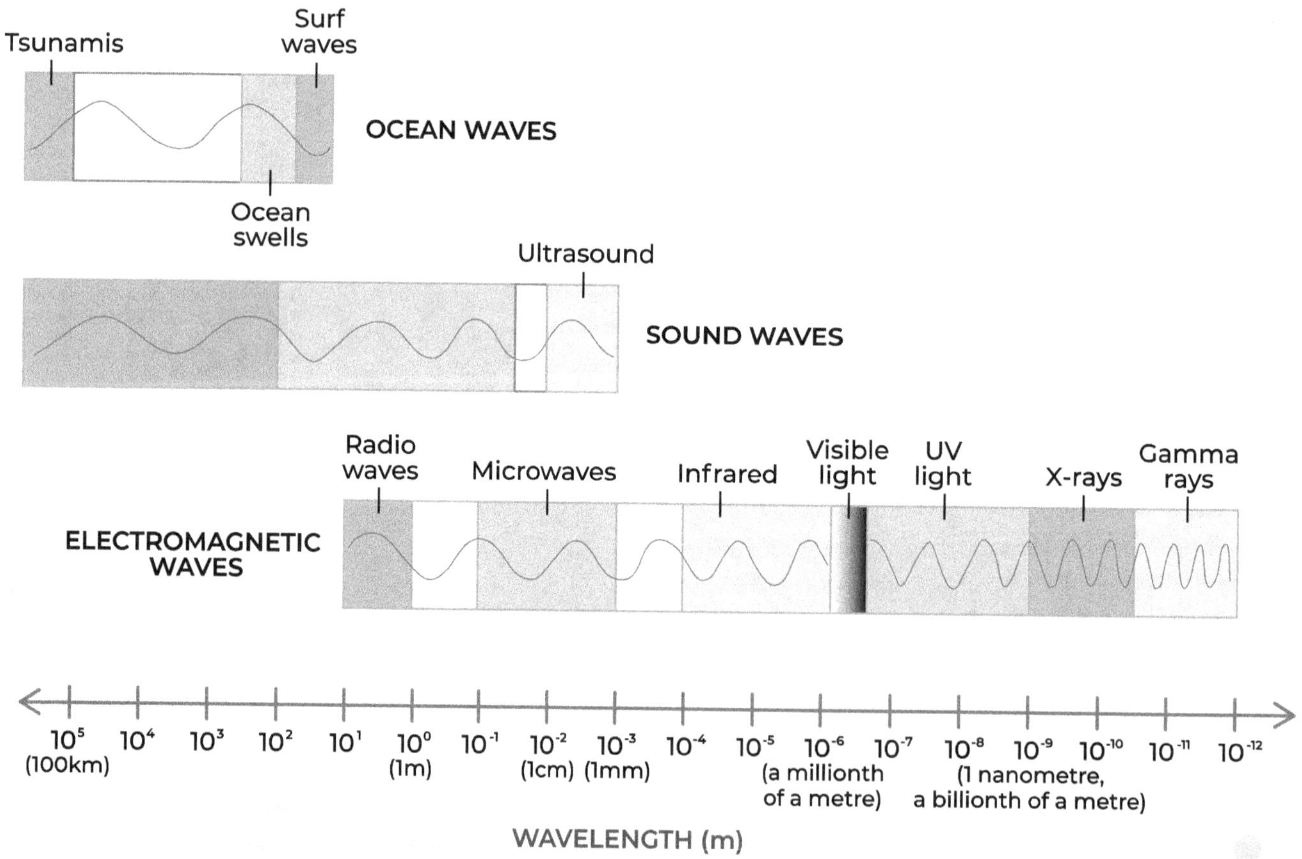

Tsunamis

Surf waves

OCEAN WAVES

Ocean swells

Ultrasound

SOUND WAVES

Radio waves Microwaves Infrared Visible light UV light X-rays Gamma rays

ELECTROMAGNETIC WAVES

10^5 (100km) 10^4 10^3 10^2 10^1 10^0 (1m) 10^{-1} 10^{-2} (1cm) 10^{-3} (1mm) 10^{-4} 10^{-5} (a millionth of a metre) 10^{-6} 10^{-7} 10^{-8} (1 nanometre, a billionth of a metre) 10^{-9} 10^{-10} 10^{-11} 10^{-12}

WAVELENGTH (m)

1. What kind of wave can be used to look inside our bodies?

    A. Microwave

    B. X-ray

    C. Sound wave

    D. Gamma ray

2. In physical science, waves are the way that .... travels.

    A. Speed

    B. Wavelength

    C. Energy

    D. Water

3. The speed that a wave travels is known as what?

    A. Wavelength

    B. Light

    C. Heat

    D. Sound

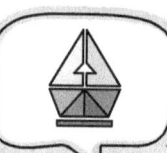
Yesterday, you learned that some forms of energy travel in waves and that the speed at which they travel is known as wavelength. Today you will explore and model how waves move.

Directions: Read each text below and complete the activity. Then answer the questions that follow.

Watery Waves: Part 1

Fill a large plastic container or even a small kiddie pool with water outside. Wait until the water is very still and then gently hit the water quickly with one finger 5 times at one side of the container. Notice the waves that originate from where you tap the water. Notice how the waves travel.

1. Were the waves large or small?

    A. Large

    B. Small

Watery Waves: Part 2

Using the same container of water, wait until the water is completely still and then hit the water quickly with your whole palm 5 times at one side of the container. Notice the waves that originate from where you tap the water. Notice how the waves travel.

2. Were the waves large or small compared to the waves you make in Part 1?

    A. Large

    B. Small

3. Where do the waves originate from in both Part 1 and Part 2?

....

....

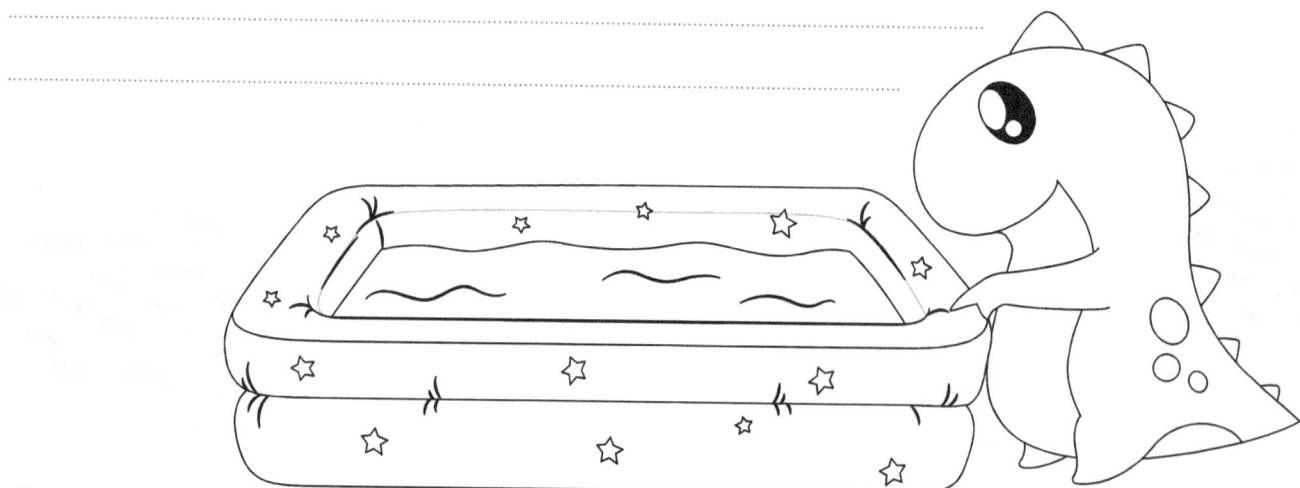

Clay Waves

Take some clay or playdough and form 3 or 4 waves. They should look similar to the image shown here.

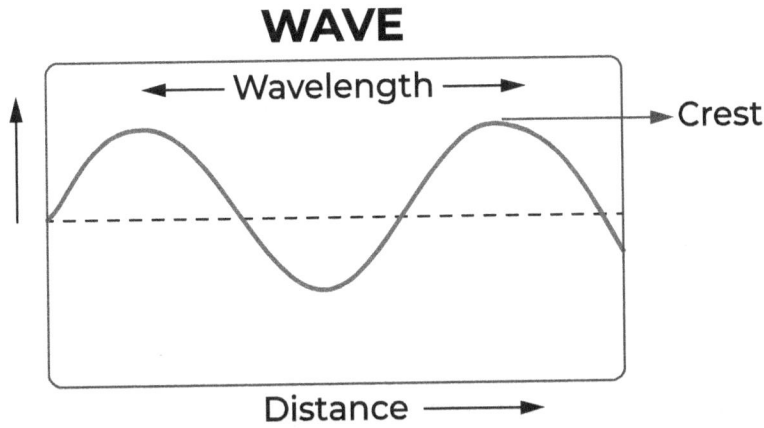

The highest point on the wave is called the **crest**. Place a toothpick on any wave crests that you have made. The distance between two crests of two waves is called the **wavelength**. The smaller the distance between two waves, the faster the wave is traveling.

4. Where on your waves did you place the toothpick?

....

....

5. If you made a 2nd model of waves so that the waves were spaced out much further than your first model, would that wave be going faster or slower than the model you made first?

   A. Faster

   B. Slower

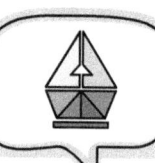

Modeling Waves
EXPLAINING THE TOPIC

Yesterday, you explored different ways that energy can be converted from one type to another. Today you will explain what you learned.

Directions: Read each text below. Then answer the questions that follow.

Watery Waves: Part 1

You discovered that when you gently touch water, small waves are made that originate from the point where you touch the water.

1. Do you think these waves have a crest that is high or not very high?

    A. High

    B. Not very high

2. If you did not touch the water at all, would waves occur?

    A. Yes

    B. No

Watery Waves: Part 2

You discovered that when you forcefully touch water, larger waves are made that originate from the point where you make contact with the water.

3. Do you think these waves have a crest that is high or not very high compared to the waves in Part 1?

    A. High

    B. Not very high

Clay Waves

You discovered that the crest of a wave is its highest point and that the distance between two crests is the wavelength. You also learned that the more distance there is between two wave crests, the slower that wave is traveling.

4. Can two waves have the same height/ crest but be different speeds? If you aren't sure, try making it out of the clay! Make two sets of waves with clay that both have waves with crests of 3 inches. Make the waves have a distance of 2 inches apart in one model but 5 inches apart in the other model.

    A. Yes

    B. No

You have spent a few days learning about waves and how their speed is determined by their shape. Today you will make a bigger model of a wave using a jump rope and a friend.

Materials:

1. A roll of butcher or art paper - white is best
2. Tape
3. Colored pencils
4. A long jump rope
5. A heavy chair
6. A friend, sibling or parent
7. A meter stick

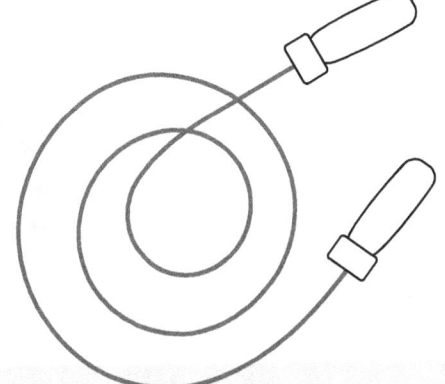

Procedure:

1. Find an open wall and tape a few rows of butcher paper to cover it completely. The paper should overlap to make sure you aren't going to get any pencil on the wall. The paper should ideally be a foot or two higher than you.

2. Tie one end of the jump rope to a chair and place it towards the edge of one side of the paper. The rope should be tied at the same height on the chair as where your hand is when you hold it down by your side.

3. Hold the other end of the rope and stand opposite the chair so that you are towards the other side of the paper. The jump rope should be stretched out right in front of the paper and so that there is one level line between the chair and your hand at your side.

4. In one motion, bring your arm up and then down. You will see a "wave" move from your arm towards the chair. Do this a few times in a row to make a series of waves while your partner is watching and then have them mark where they think the crest is on the paper with a colored pencil.

5. Take a step or two towards the chair. The rope will droop towards or touch the ground now. Complete step #4 again. Have your partner mark the crest of the new wave with a different colored pencil.

6. Lastly, stay in the same spot and shorten the rope so that there is one straight line or rope again like you started with. Make a series of waves and have your partner mark the crest of the new wave with a different colored pencil.

Follow-Up Questions:

1. What does the rope make when you whip it up and down with your arm?

....

....

....

2. What was your partner marking on the paper?

....

....

....

....

....

....

....

Yesterday, you experimented with modeling waves using a jump rope. Today you will elaborate on what you learned about the crest and wavelength of waves.

Directions: Read and answer each question below.

1. When was the crest of the wave highest?

   ....

   ....

2. When you stepped in towards the chair during step #5, what did you shorten?

   A. The crest

   B. The chair

   C. The wavelength

3. When the wavelength is shorter, the wave was going ....

   A. Faster

   B. Slower

4. When you pulled the rope shorter in step #6, did the crest of the wave get taller or shorter than it was in step #5?

   A. Shorter

   B. Taller

5. Besides making the rope longer or shorter, how could you speed up your wavelength?

WEEK 6

Physical Science

Perception Of Light

4-PS4-2

 Develop a model to describe that light reflecting from objects and entering the eye allows objects to be seen.

Directions: Read the text below. Then answer the questions that follow.

Light & Reflection

Last week you learned all about how energy can move in waves. One type of wave that energy can travel in is **light**. Almost all of the natural light we experience on Earth comes from the sun, a huge ball of gas which gives off large amounts of energy. Light can also be created from electricity in your home when you turn on a lamp or fire when you burn a candle. Light allows us to see everything around us. When light **reflects** off of objects, or bounces off of them, it enters our eyes. Our brain makes sense of this information and as a result we can see the world around us! This week we will explore how light and our sense of sight are related.

1. The way that light moves can best be described as a what?

   A. Circle

   B. Line

   C. Blast

   D. Wave

2. When light reflects off of an object, what part of your body does that light enter?

   A. Eyes

   B. Mouth

   C. Skin

   D. Ears

3. True or False: Light is a type of energy?

   A. True

   B. False

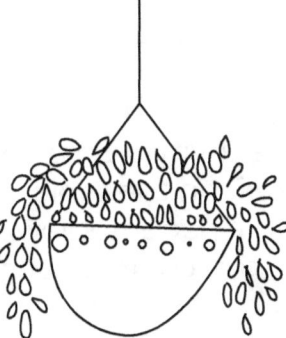

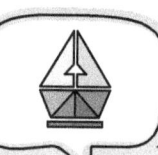
Yesterday, you learned that our eyes use the light reflected off objects in order to see. Today we will explore this idea.

Directions: Read each text below and complete the activity. Then answer the questions that follow.

Turn On The Lights

This works best at night and with a parent. Go into your bedroom and make sure all the shades are drawn and all of the lights are off so it is as dark as can be. Ask a parent to light a candle in the center of the room. Notice how much of your room you can see. Now turn on the lights in your room and again notice how much of your room you can see.

1. Was it easier to see more objects in your room when a candle was lit or when you turned on the lights in your room?

   A. Candle

   B. Lights

Rainbows At Night

This activity works best on a somewhat sunny day. Take this workbook outside and place it on the table in front of you right before dusk so that the image of the rainbow on this page is showing. Every 10-20 minutes, take a look at the rainbow and notice how the colors change until it is dark outside. You are watching to see how sunset changes the look of the rainbow.

2. When was it easiest to see all of the colors of the rainbow?

....

....

....

Mirror, Mirror

This activity should be done inside in a room that is not too bright. Take a small mirror and prop it up against a book on the floor so that it stands up facing you. Sit to the right side of the mirror so that it is still in front but offset. Take a flashlight and shine it at the mirror. Look around the room to see where the reflection of the light is - it will look like a spot of light and will likely be somewhere opposite the mirror.

3. What does the mirror do to the light from the flashlight?

....

....

4. Does the light bounce back towards the flashlight?

....

....

....

Yesterday, you explored different ways that light and our eyes interact. Today you will explain what you experienced in the activities you competed.

Directions: Read each text below. Then answer the questions that follow.

Turn On The Lights

You discovered that it was easier to see more of your room when it was lit with electric lights than with a candle.

1. Do you think the candle or the electric lights in your room gave off more energy?

   A. Candle

   B. Electric Lights

2. Explain why you chose your answer for question #1.

   ....

   ....

   ....

   ....

Rainbows At Night

You discovered that as the sun sets, the image of a rainbow changes until you can't see it any longer.

3. What happened to the colors of the rainbow as the sun set?

   ....

   ....

   ....

   ....

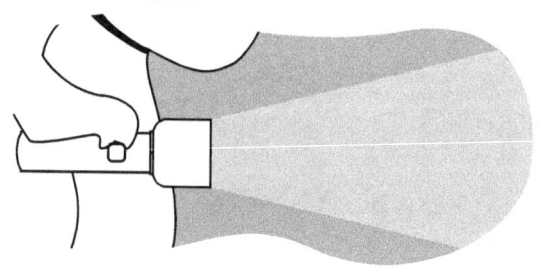

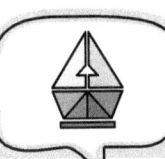
Mirror, Mirror

You discovered that the light from a flashlight bounces off of a mirror and does not reflect directly back at the flashlight but at a different place in the room.

4. If you wanted to have the light reflect right back towards you and the flashlight, where would you need to sit in relation to the mirror? Feel free to draw your answer if it is easier.

....

....

....

....

You have spent a few days learning about how light reflects off of different objects and how that relates to our sense of sight. Today you will experiment with these concepts further.

Materials:

1. A protractor
2. Tape
3. A pencil
4. A piece of blank white copy paper
5. A small mirror (it should be smaller than your protractor is across)
6. A laser pointer

Procedure:

1. Tape your protractor to the center of your white piece of paper.
2. Place your small mirror on the paper right at the long, flat edge of the protractor so that the mirror is facing the curved side. You can prop the mirror up with an object so it is standing straight up against the protractor.
3. Dim the lights in the room so it is easier to see the lazer.
4. Take the laser pointer and place it at the 40° mark on the protractor and turn it on. Notice the angle that the laser reflects off the mirror and write down what other number of the protractor the light reflects through. Record this in the table below.
5. Repeat step #3 by moving the laser pointer to the 10° mark and then the 90° mark and recording the reflection angle below in the table.
6. Pick any angle and record your finding in the last row of the table.

Placement of Laser Pointer	Angle Laser Reflected Off Mirror
40°	
10°	
90°	
You choose!	

Yesterday, you experimented with reflecting light off of a mirror at different angles. Today you will elaborate on your observations and the data you recorded.

Directions: Read and answer each question below.

1. Why do you think the laser only made one line when you placed it at the 90° mark?

....

....

2. Which place or number of the protractor made the widest angle when it reflected the laser?

....

....

3. In order for you to see the laser pointer, some of the light from the laser had to reflect into what?

....

....

4. If you used a laser pointer that was a different color, do you think this experiment would still work? Why or why not?

....

....

5. If you used a different surface than a mirror, say a piece of cardboard, do you think this experiment would still work? Why or why not?

....

....

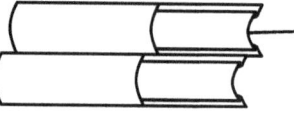

WEEK 7

Physical Science

Information Transfer

4-PS4-3

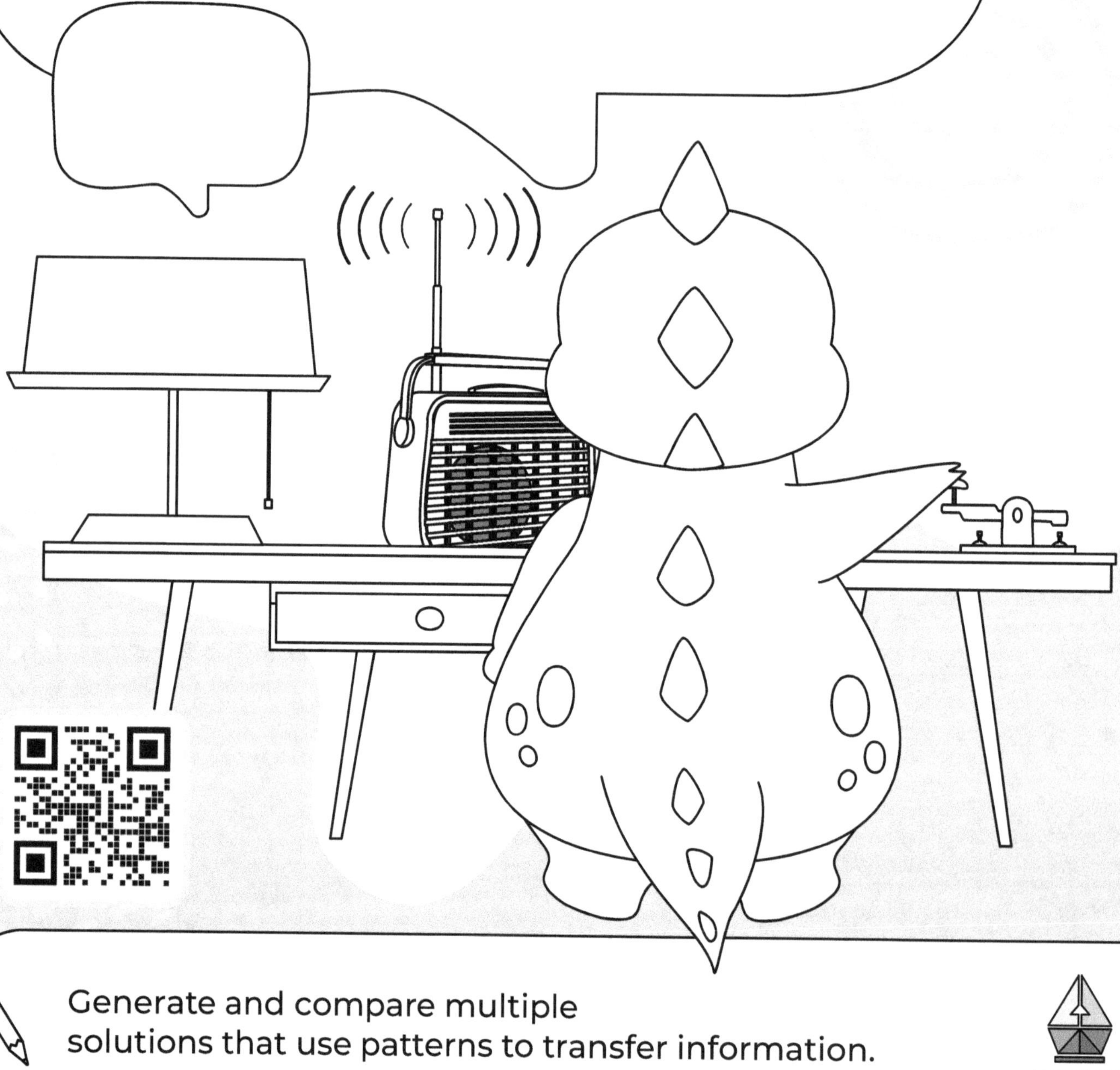

Generate and compare multiple solutions that use patterns to transfer information.

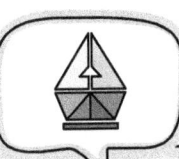
Directions: Read the text below. Then answer the questions that follow.

Sending Information With Energy

Information about our world is all around us. When light waves are present, that energy can be used by us to see things like this workbook in front of you. When sound waves are heard, we can hear someone talking to us or music being played. Our senses pick up on lots of different kinds of energy and that energy can be understood in different ways. Today we will talk about **information transfer** which is how we use energy to communicate with each other and get information about the world around us.

1. Light energy helps us get information through what sense?

   A. Sound

   B. Touch

   C. Sight

   D. Taste

2. What kind of waves can be heard?

   A. Gamma rays

   B. X-rays

   C. Light

   D. Sound

3. What is it called when energy moves from one place to another place?

   A. Information transfer

   B. Waves

   C. Sending

   D. Understanding

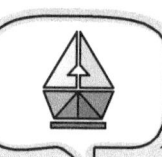
Yesterday, you learned how energy can be used to communicate and understand the world through information transfer. Today you will explore this with a friend, sibling or parent.

Directions: Read each text below and complete the activity. Then answer the questions that follow.

Secret Message

Stand on the opposite side of a large room or space from your partner. Whisper "There is a small goat in the closet" as quietly as you can. Ask them what they think you said. Now, loudly say the phrase "I wish we had a snack to eat" and ask them what they think they heard you say.

1. Which phrase was easier for your partner to hear?

   A. There is a small goat in the closet
   B. I wish we had a snack to eat

Entertaining Information

Turn on the TV and put on your favorite show for a moment. The show was made in a different place than your home. The show is being sent to your TV, and other TVs, all around the world. If you switch the channel, a different show will appear that was made in a different place and at a different time.

2. What type of energy powers your television?

   A. Electricity
   B. Sound
   C. Light

Traveling Smells

Ask your partner to go across the room from you and peel an orange. As they do this, stay where you are and inhale through your nose every few moments until you can smell the scent of the orange.

3. What information was your nose detecting?

....

....

4. Do you see how information was transferred from the orange to your nose without you having to actually be next the orange?

    A. Yes

    B. No

Yesterday, you explored different ways that information can be transferred between people and objects. Today you will explain what you learned about information transfer in more detail.

Directions: Read each text below. Then answer the questions that follow.

Secret Message

You discovered that it was easier to hear a secret message that was said loudly as opposed to whispered.

1. What type of energy were you creating when you said messages to your partner yesterday?

    A. Light

    B. Sound

2. When you speak loudly do you think you are making more or less energy than when you whisper?

    A. More

    B. Less

Entertaining Information

You discovered that electricity is the energy used to power a TV so you can watch it.

3. What type of energy needs to go into your eye in order for you to be able to watch the show?

    A. Electricity

    B. Sound

    C. Light

Traveling Smells

You discovered that information in the form of scent is transferred from the orange to your nose when the orange is peeled.

4. If someone was baking cookies in a different room of the house, could you still smell the cookies even if you could not see them?

    A. Yes

    B. No

You have spent a few days learning about how information can be transferred in many different ways including with electricity, sound, smell and lightwaves or sight. Today you will explore how to send a message with Morse Code using light.

Materials:

1. A partner

Procedure:

1. Look at the Morse Code chart pictured here.

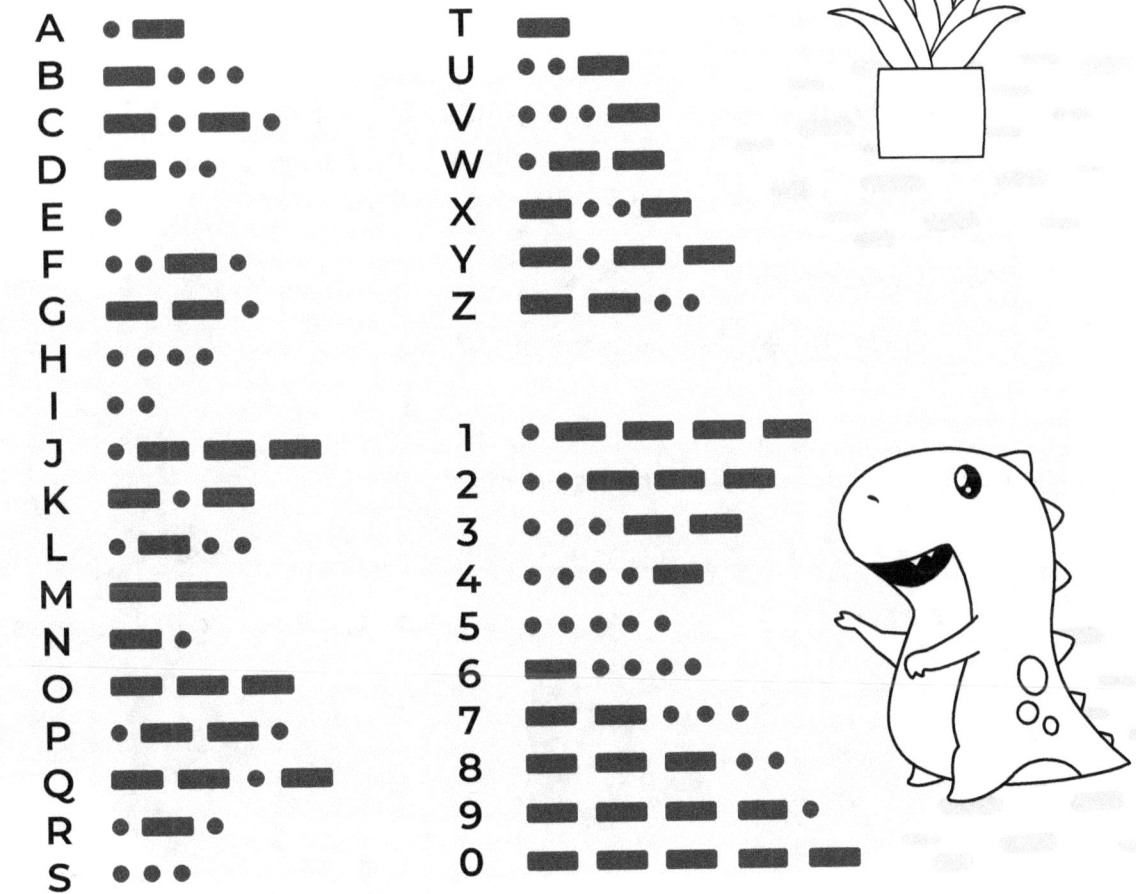

You can write morse code with dots and dashes. You can also say "dot" and "dash" in order to communicate morse code to someone else through sound. There are special machines that were created to send morse code over long distances with tones that were either long or short to represent dots (short tones) and dashes (longer tones).

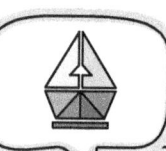
2. Look at the chart and in the space below write the word "TIGER" in morse code with dots and dashes. ....

3. Now that you know how to spell "tiger" in morse code, you will signal it to your partner with your voice. Explain that they should write down a dot when you say "dot" and a dash when you say "dash". Read through your code as it is written above.

4. Once they have received your code, let them try to translate it using the chart on this page - make sure these directions are covered so they don't figure out your secret word. They can also look up a morse code on the internet and have that in front of them instead.

5. When they have the word, ask them to tell you. If it is incorrect, try again or help them see where they might have made a mistake.

6. Once you both understand how to use the chart, try sending secret messages to each other! Try a whole sentence! Make sure between words to leave a brief pause of silence to indicate a space between words.

Follow-Up Questions:

1. What word represents this symbol? —

....

2. Write the word "Heart" in morse code.

....

3. Write the phrase "A tiny mouse" in morse code. Use "/" to indicate a space between words.

....

....

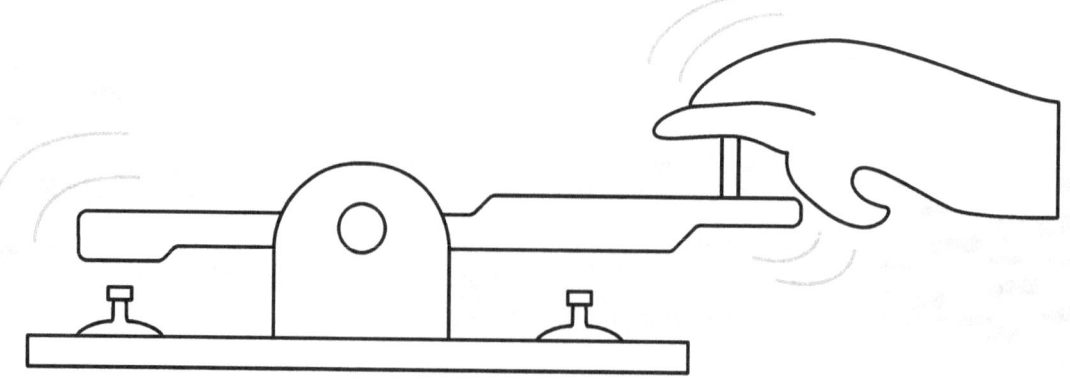

Yesterday, you experimented with morse code and how it can be used to send messages secretly. Today you will elaborate on your experiences using this type of code.

Directions: Read and answer each question below.

1. What type of energy was used when you transferred a message to your partner in step #3 of the procedure yesterday?

2. Is it harder to translate a word or a whole sentence? Why?

3. If a person was deaf, could they still use morse code?

4. Is the transfer of information using different kinds of energy and signals useful?

   A. Yes

   B. No

WEEK 8

Life Science

Animal Structures & Their Functions

4-LS1-1

Construct an argument that animals have internal and external structures that function to support survival, growth, behavior, and reproduction.

ARGOPREP

Directions: Read the text below. Then answer the questions that follow.

Form Fits Function

Take a moment and look at your hand. Notice how it has long, thin fingers which are perfect for picking up things. Notice how you have fingerprints - these are to create traction so you can pick up things. If you did not have fingerprints, it would be really hard to hold on to objects that you pick up. Your fingers can also bend to wrap around things that you want to hold.

For humans, and all other animals, the **form** of our bodies has a lot to do with how they work or how they **function**. This week we will explore different structures that are part of animals and see how they help animals live, survive and thrive in their environment.

1. How would you describe the form of your fingers?

   A. Short and round

   B. Long and thin

   C. Stiff and wide

   D. Rubbery and huge

2. What is the function of a fingerprint?

   A. To help you pick things up easier

   B. To leave a mark on things

   C. To feel things

   D. There is no function

3. What do the different structures of animals help them do?

   A. Live

   B. Survive

   C. Thrive

   D. All of the above

Yesterday, you learned how form fits function - or in other words, how the structures that are part of animals help them live and survive. Today you will explore this topic further.

Directions: Read each text below and complete the activity. Then answer the questions that follow.

A Family Pet

Take a moment and notice the fur on your cat or dog. If you do not own a cat or dog, think about one that you have seen in your neighborhood or on TV.

1. What covers <u>most</u> of a cat or dog's body?

   A. Whiskers

   B. Claws

   C. Teeth

   D. Fur

2. What do you think the function of fur is? How does it help a cat or dog?

....

....

Darwin's Finches

When naturalist Charles Darwin went to the Galapagos Islands, he noticed that each species of finch had a different beak. If a bird ate nuts, it had a big, thick beak to crack the nuts open. If the bird drank nectar it had a long, thin beak to use like a straw when drinking out of flowers.

3. Different species of finches have differences in what structure?

   A. Feathers

   B. Beaks

   C. Talons

   D. Eyes

Hollow Bones

Many species of birds have evolved to have hollow bones. This means that they are very light and that their skeletons weigh very little even for very large birds. We humans on the other hand do not have hollow bones and our skeletons are therefore much heavier.

4. Can you think of one thing that makes humans and birds different? Hint: think about how we move and travel and how birds move and travel.

....

....

....

....

....

Yesterday, you explored different structures that different animals have and what their functions are. Today you will explain how the forms of structures in animals help them live.

Directions: Read each text below. Then answer the questions that follow.

A Family Pet

You discovered that cats and dogs are covered in fur which helps them stay warm, especially when it is cold in their environment.

1. Do you think a dog that had no fur would be able to live in a very cold climate such as Alaska?

    A. Yes

    B. No

Darwin's Finches

You discovered that different species of birds called finches have different shaped beaks depending on what they eat.

2. Do you think a bird with a long, thin beak used to drink nectar would survive in an environment where the only food is hard, thick nuts?

    A. Yes

    B. No

Hollow Bones

You discovered that birds have hollow bones which make them very light. This makes it easier for them to fly.

3. What is another structure on a bird's body that helps them fly? You can do some research on the Internet if you are not sure.

    ....

    ....

    ....

    ....

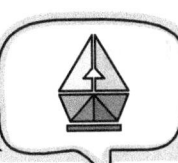
You have spent a few days learning about the structures that are part of an animal's body help them do certain things or live certain ways. Today you will research the function of different interesting animal structures.

Background:

A few animals are listed below in the table. A specific structure that they have is also listed on the table. Use the Internet and research how they used this structure and what its purpose is. Fill in the chart as you go.

Data Table:

Animal	Structure	Function
Skunk	Scent gland	
Wolf	Canine teeth	
Zebra fish	Swim bladder	
Jellyfish	Nematocysts	

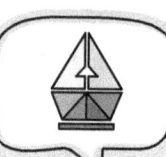
Follow-Up Questions:

1. Which structure is the most interesting to you?

....

....

....

2. Which structure do you (a human) also have?

....

....

....

Yesterday, you researched why different animals have different structures and what they use them for. Today you will elaborate on your findings.

Directions: Read and answer each question below.

1. Do you think it would make sense for a wolf to evolve a swim bladder? Why or why not?

_____

_____

_____

2. Do you see how the environment influences what types of structures an animal has?

A. Yes

B. No

3. Which structures on the table are used by animals to defend themselves from predators?

_____

_____

_____

4. Which structure or structures do you wish you also had?

_____

_____

_____

_____

_____

_____

Life Science

Plant Structures & Their Functions

4-LS1-1

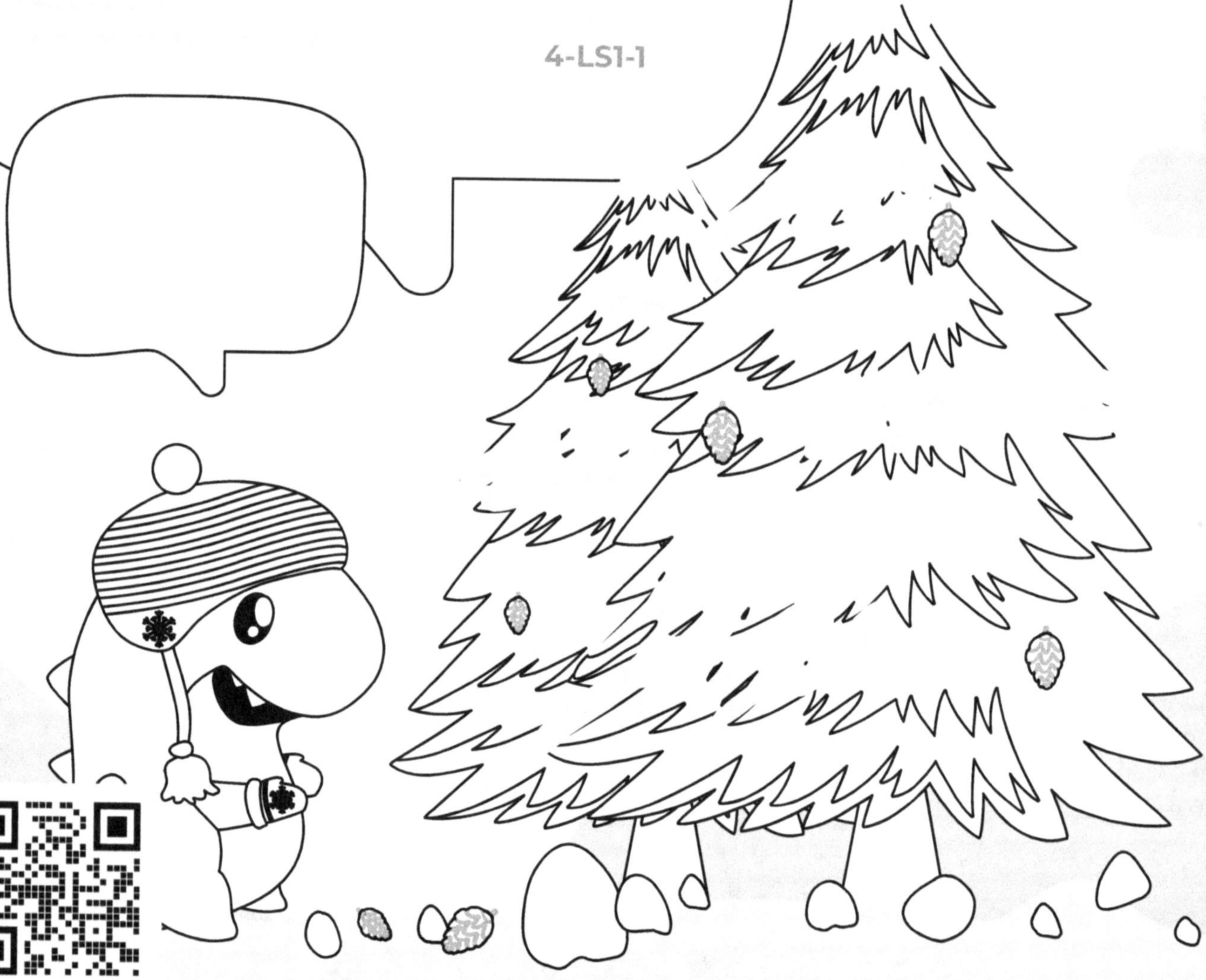

Construct an argument that plants have internal and external structures that function to support survival, growth, behavior, and reproduction.

Directions: Read the text below. Then answer the questions that follow.

" Form Fits Function...Again!

Last week you learned that animals have different structures that have specific functions. These functions have a lot to do with the environment that the animal lives in. But did you know that plants have specific structures and functions too? If you think about it, plants are also living organisms and also need to respond to their environment. Plants can have predators the same as animals can, do they have evolved structures that help them defend themselves such as spines and thorns. Plants need to reproduce and make new plants so they have flowers and seeds. This week we will focus on plant structures and functions. "

1. Do plants have structures with specific functions?

A. Yes

B. No

C. Unsure

2. What structure helps plants defend themselves against predators?

A. Flowers

B. Pollen

C. Thorns

D. Roots

3. What is the function of seeds?

A. To make food

B. To reproduce

C. To smell good

D. To make energy

Yesterday, you learned how form fits function - or in other words, how the structures that are part of plants help them live and survive. Today you will explore this topic further.

Directions: Read each text below and complete the activity. Then answer the questions that follow.

Thin & Flat

Many plants have leaves so that they can make their own energy through the process of photosynthesis - plants turn the sun's energy into sugar. In order to do this, plants make leaves that are big and flat so they can capture as much of the sun's energy as possible. The leaves are always above ground because that is where the sunlight is.

1. If plants grew leaves below ground, where their roots are, would they be able to use leaves for the process of photosynthesis?

    A. Yes

    B. No

Yucky Taste

Many plants taste very bitter when they are eaten. They taste this way because they make chemicals which warn potential predators that eat this plant can make them sick. Once an animal takes a bite out of this plant, they learn to never eat that plant again or they will get sick.

2. What is the function of a plant making chemicals so that it tastes bitter?

    A. For fun

    B. To help make seeds

    C. A warning to predators

    D. For photosynthesis

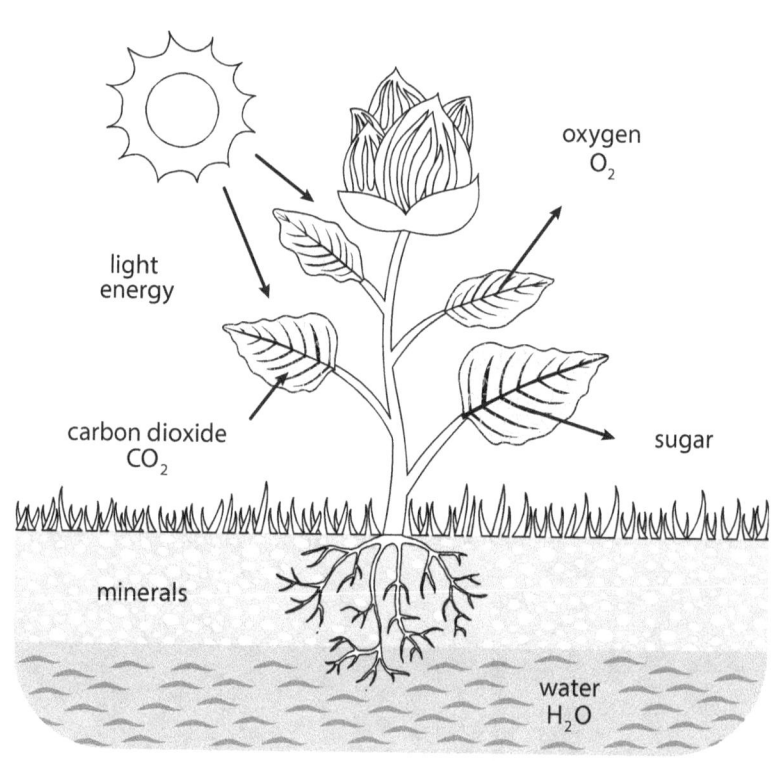

Hollow Cacti

Cacti and other succulents live in very dry areas like deserts. These plants are also mostly hollow inside. Desert environments do not get much rain. When it does rain, cacti and succulents quickly absorb and store as much water as they can in their hollow insides. This means they can survive off of the water stored inside of them even if there is no rain for a very long time.

3. Do you see how storing water inside of their hollow structures helps cacti and succulents survive in dry, desert environments?

    A. Yes

    B. No

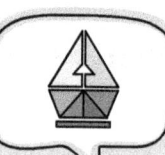

Plant Structures & Their Functions

EXPLAINING THE TOPIC

Yesterday, you explored different structures that different plants have and what their functions are. Today you will explain how the forms of structures in plants help them survive and thrive.

Directions: Read each text below. Then answer the questions that follow.

Thin & Flat

You discovered that leaves are used to help plants make energy and that they would not be very useful structures if they grew underground.

1. What is the name of the process that plants use their leaves for?

   A. Sugar

   B. Sunlight

   C. Photosynthesis

   D. Growing

Yucky Taste

You discovered that some plants taste bitter in order to warn potential predators that the plant will make them sick if they eat it.

2. What makes the plant taste bitter to the animal which eats it?

   A. Smells

   B. Thorns

   C. Leaves

   D. Chemicals

Hollow Cacti

You discovered that succulents and cacti are hollow so they can store water in dry, desert areas whenever it does rain.

3. Do you think a plant which lives in water, such as a lilypad, is hollow for water storage? Why or why not?

....

....

....

You have spent a few days learning about the structures that are part of plants and which help them do certain things or live certain ways. Today you will research the function of different interesting plant structures.

Background:

A few plants are listed below in the table. A specific structure that they have is also listed on the table. Use the Internet and research how they use this structure and what its purpose is. Fill in the chart as you go.

Data Table:

Plant	Structure	Function
Willow Tree	Roots	
Orchid	Flower	
Cedar Tree	Lignin	
Pine Tree	Pine cones	

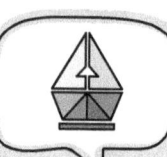
Follow-Up Questions:

1. Which structure is the most interesting to you?

....

....

....

....

....

2. Which structure or structures are used for reproduction (to grow new plants)?

....

....

....

....

....

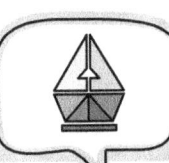
Yesterday, you researched why different animals have different structures and what they use them for. Today you will elaborate on your findings.

Directions: Read and answer each question below.

1. Why do you think that trees have lignin, but a small plant like grass does not have lignin?

_____

_____

_____

2. Do you see that plants have specific structures with specific functions?

A. Yes

B. No

3. If a tree had no roots, what resource would it have a hard time getting?

_____

_____

_____

4. Research a few other types of flowers besides orchids - which one is most beautiful to you and why?

_____

_____

_____

_____

Life Science

The Senses

4-LS1-2

Use a model to describe that animals receive different types of information through their senses and process the information in their brain.

ARGOPREP

Directions: Read the text below. Then answer the questions that follow.

Your Five Senses

Take an orange and set it on the table in front of you. Notice what it looks like - its shape and color. Hold it in your hand and notice how it feels - its texture, weight and temperature. Peel it and sniff the rind. Take a bite of a piece of it and notice its taste. Listen to how it sounds as you chew it in your mouth. You've just used all five of your senses to experience this orange!

Yoru five senses are **touch, taste, smell, hearing and sight.** Our senses allow us to receive different information about our surroundings and interact with the world around us. This week we will explore all five of your senses and discover how wonderful they are!

1. When you sniffed the orange, what sense did you use?

   A. Touch

   B. Taste

   C. Smell

   D. Sight

2. When you noticed the orange's texture, which sense did you use?

   A. Touch

   B. Taste

   C. Smell

   D. Hearing

3. How many different senses do you have?

   A. Two

   B. Three

   C. Four

   D. Five

Yesterday, you learned that you have five senses which help you explore the world around you. Today you will explore your senses in more depth.

Directions: Read each text below and complete the activity. Then answer the questions that follow.

A Delightful Smell

Ask a parent to toast a piece of bread and then place it in front of you while your eyes are closed. Inhale deeply and notice the smell of the toast.

1. What body part do you use for your sense of smell?

_____

_____

_____

Mysterious Jelly Beans

Have a friend or parent give you one jelly bean at a time with your eyes closed. Pop it in your mouth and try to identify the flavor of the jelly bean without looking at it. Have your partner mark how many flavors you identify correctly.

2. What sense do you need to use in order to determine the flavor of the jelly bean?

_____

_____

_____

3. If you were able to look at the jelly beans while doing this activity, what other sense would you be using?

_____

_____

_____

_____

A Game Of Telephone

Gather a few friends or family members and play a couple rounds of the game telephone. One person will choose a short phrase and then whisper it to the person next to them. That person will then whisper what they thought they heard to the next person. This will repeat until the message is said to the last person at which time they will say out loud what they think the original phrase was.

4. What sense are you using in order to play this game?

....

....

....

....

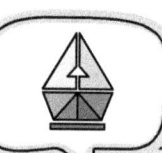
Yesterday, you explored different structures that different plants have and what their functions are. Today you will explain how the forms of structures in plants help them survive and thrive.

Directions: Read each text below. Then answer the questions that follow.

A Delightful Smell

You discovered that you use your nose in order to use your sense of smell.

1. Were you able to smell the toast even though your eyes were closed?

   A. Yes

   B. No

Mysterious Jelly Beans

You discovered that you could identify some flavors of jelly beans correctly even if you could not see the colors of them.

2. Would using your sense of touch in this activity help you identify their flavor at all? Why or why not?

A Game Of Telephone

You discovered that you use your sense of hearing in order to play the game of telephone.

3. Which types of sounds are easier to hear?

   A. Quiet sounds

   B. Loud sounds

4. What part of your body is used for hearing?

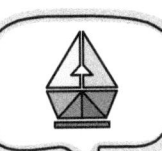
You have spent a few days learning about the five senses. Today you will experiment with your sense of touch by trying to identify mystery substances and materials. Make sure you have a partner for this activity.

Materials:

1. A box with a lid such as a showbox
2. Scissors
3. A bandana or a blindfold
4. 6-8 different items from around your house (they should be able to fit in the box easily and be safe to hold)

Procedure:

1. Cut a small hole in the lid of the box so that your hand can fit through the hole.
2. Have your blindfold you.
3. Have your partner place one item in the box at a time and have you place your hand in the hole of the box and feel the object. Feel free to rotate it around in your hand. Try to identify the object.
4. Have your partner write down if you got the object correct or not and then place a new object in the box. Do this once with all of the objects.

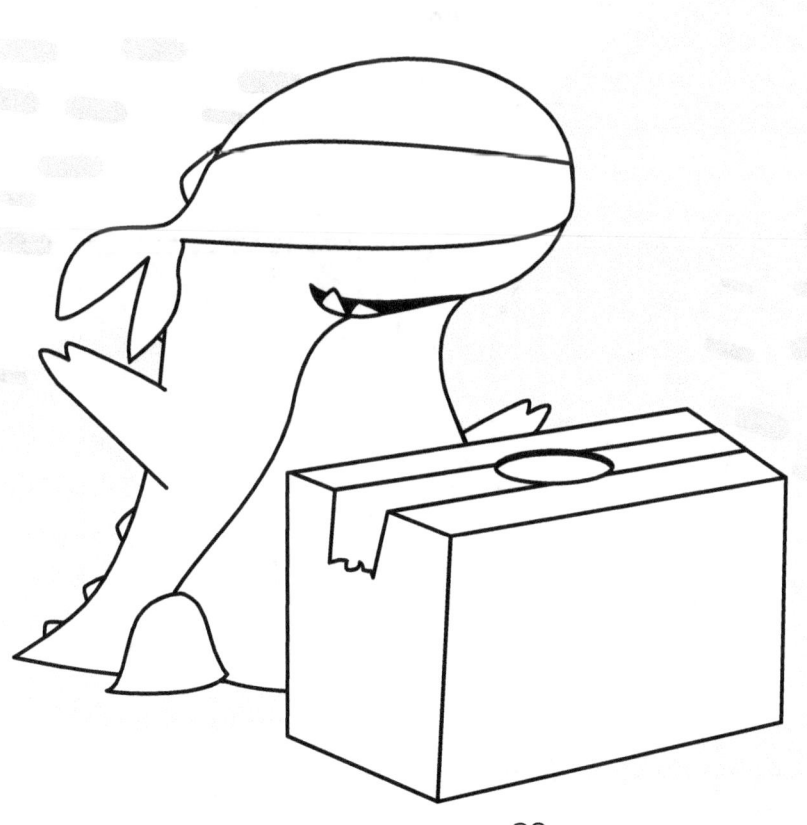

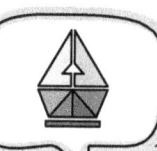
Follow-Up Questions:

1. What sense were you using in this activity?

....

....

2. How many objects did you identify correctly?

....

....

3. What object was easiest for you to identify? Why?

....

....

4. Were you able to identify the weight of an object using your hand?

    A. Yes

    B. No

5. Were you able to identify the smell of an object in this activity?

    A. Yes

    B. No

Yesterday, you experimented with your sense of touch by identifying different mystery items in a box. Today you will elaborate on the activity and what you learned all week about the five senses.

Directions: Read and answer each question below.

1. Is it hard to identify some objects with only your sense of touch?

2. What are some characteristics about an object that you can learn about using your sense of touch?

3. If a person is deaf, meaning they cannot hear, what sense might they use to communicate with other people? If you are unsure, do a bit of research online.

4. When you have a cold and your nose is really stuffy, it is often hard to taste food. Which other sense helps you with your sense of taste?

5. If you wear glasses or contact lenses, which of your senses are you helping?

WEEK 11

Life Science
Responding To Stimuli

4-LS1-2

Use a model to describe how animals process information in their brain and respond to the information in different ways.

ARGOPREP

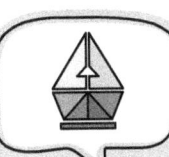
Directions: Read the text below. Then answer the questions that follow.

How Animals Respond

Animals have the ability to respond to the world around them. When the seasons change, monarch butterflies will migrate. When there are predators in the environment, prairie dogs will make calls to each other to warn them of the danger. **Stimuli** are things that change in the environment and a **response** is how the animal behaves as a result. For example, think back to the example of the prairie dogs previously mentioned. The stimuli is the predator in their environment and the response is the behavior of the prairie dogs calling to each other. This week you will learn about different ways that animals respond to stimuli in their environment and how this helps them survive.

1. Something that changes in the environment is known as what?

   A. Predator

   B. Response

   C. Stimuli

   D. Survival

2. The behavior that animals have in response to changes in their environment is known as what?

   A. Predator

   B. Response

   C. Stimuli

   D. Survival

3. When a .... is in their environment, prairie dogs will call out to each other as a warning.

   A. Stimuli

   B. Predator

   C. Response

   D. Migration

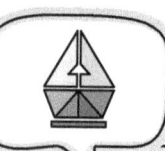
Yesterday, you learned that animals respond to stimuli in their environment. Today you will explore this idea further by completing activities.

Directions: Read each text below and complete the activity. Then answer the questions that follow.

Training An Animal

Dogs can be trained to sit, stay, lay down, and roll over just to name a few tricks. Oftentimes they learn that when they do this, they will get a small treat. Perhaps you have even taught your pet some tricks using this method!

1. What is the stimulus in this example?

   A. Sitting

   B. Treats

   C. Barking

Tadpoles In The Moonlight

When frogs are young, they spend part of their life as eggs which then hatch into small tadpoles. Some species of frogs lay eggs right before a full moon and then the eggs will hatch on the night of the full moon.

2. What is the stimulus which causes the eggs to hatch?

   A. Water

   B. Frogs

   C. Full moon

A Mosquito To Light

"Bug zappers" are electronic lights which attract insects like mosquitoes and flies and then zap the insects when they touch the light. This is a way to manage pests in your yard. Insects are known to be attracted to bright lights, especially when it is dark outside, because light helps them find their way.

3. What is the stimulus that causes insects to move towards the bug zapper?

....

....

....

....

....

....

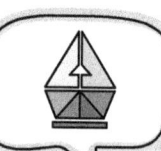
Yesterday, you explored how different animals respond to stimuli in their environment with different kinds of behavior. Today you will explain how and why they do this.

Directions: Read each text below. Then answer the questions that follow.

Training An Animal

You discovered that pets like dogs can learn tricks when they are given treats each time.

1. What are some of the behaviors a dog might have when they are given a treat?

Tadpoles In The Moonlight

You discovered that some species of frogs will lay their eggs so that tadpoles can hatch during a full moon.

2. Do frogs lay the eggs before a full moon or during a full moon?

    A. During a full moon

    B. Before a full moon

3. If the frogs laid their eggs after a full moon, when would the tadpoles hatch?

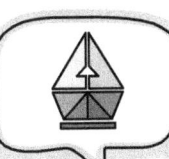
A Mosquito To Light

You discovered that insects are attracted to the light of bug zappers because they are attracted to light in their environment, especially at night.

4. If insects were not attracted to light, would a bug zapper work?

    A. Yes

    B. No

5. What is the response or the behavior that insects have to light?

....

....

....

....

....

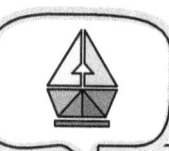
You have spent a few days learning how animals respond to their environment. Today you will experiment with these ideas and show how a chameleon might camouflage in their environment.Materials:

Materials:

1. Two piece of of fabric with two different patterns
2. Tape
3. Different colors of construction paper
4. Colored pencils
5. Scissors

Background:

Chameleons are lizards which have the incredible ability to camouflage in their environment. They do this to avoid predators. They have special cells in their skin which change colors in order to match the colors in their environment. Look up some videos and pictures on the internet of them doing this behavior. It is such an amazing thing to see! Do you wish you could camouflage like a chameleon?

Procedure:

1. Tape your two pieces of fabric to a wall. Take a moment to look at all the colors and patterns on the fabric.

2. Now use the colored paper to make a chameleon of your own! It should have similar colors and patterns to one of the fabrics so it blends in.

3. Once you have your chameleon, place it in front of the other fabric. Notice that it does not blend in as well to this fabric. If you want to and you have time, make another chameleon that blends in with the second piece of fabric.

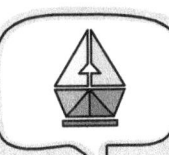
Follow-Up Questions:

1. What are the stimuli in the chameleon's environment?

....

....

2. What is the behavior that you are trying to recreate with your paper chameleon?

....

....

3. Did your chameleon blend in better with the first piece of fabric or the second piece of fabric better?

   A. First piece of fabric

   B. Second piece of fabric

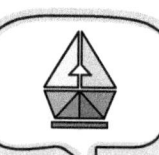
Yesterday, you experimented with making a paper chameleon that could blend in with different fabrics. Today you will elaborate on that activity.

Directions: Read and answer each question below.

1. Do you think it is helpful for a chameleon to be able to camouflage?

    A. Yes

    B. No

2. Did your chameleon blend in perfectly with the fabric background or were there some differences?

    ....

    ....

3. Why does it benefit a chameleon to be able to blend in with its surroundings?

    ....

    ....

4. What is a stimulus that you respond to in your environment? How do you behave when that stimulus is in your environment?

    ....

    ....

5. Think back to last week and how you use your senses to interact with the environment. Do you see how your senses help you pick up on stimuli?

    A. Yes

    B. No

WEEK 12

Earth & Space Science

Earth's Changes Over Time

4-ESS1-1

Identify evidence from patterns in rock formations and fossils in rock layers to support an explanation for changes in a landscape over time.

ARGOPREP

Directions: Read the text below. Then answer the questions that follow.

The Layers In Earth's Crust

If you've ever been to a canyon such as the Grand Canyon, you may have noticed that there are layers of different colors and textures in the rock. If you were able to dig a deep hole into the ground, you would notice that there are also layers in the ground. The top layer might be grass and below that soil. Below the soil you'd likely find layers of clay or even solid rock. The layers in Earth's crust, the top most part of the planet, are called **stratum**. The older a layer of stratum is, the lower it will be in Earth's crust. This means that newer stratum are closer to Earth's surface. This means that if a fossil is found in a particular layer of stratum, and scientists know how old the rocks in that layer are, they can know how long ago that fossil is from! This is how we know about how long ago different species of animal, including dinosaurs, roamed the Earth before going extinct. How cool is that?

1. What are the layers in Earth's crust called?

   A. Stratum

   B. Striated

   C. Rocks

   D. Fossils

2. The _____ a layer of stratum is, the closer it will be to Earth's surface.

   A. Heavier

   B. Thicker

   C. Older

   D. Newer

3. True or false: the age of a fossil can be determined if you know what layer of rock it was found in.

   A. True

   B. False

Yesterday, you learned that stratum are layers of Earth and that older layers of stratum are found deeper in Earth's crust. Today you will complete some activities which highlight this idea.

Directions: Read each text below and complete the activity. Then answer the questions that follow.

Colorful Stratum

Get thick paint (such as acrylic) and make sure you have the colors yellow, red and blue. Take a paper plate and place a blob of yellow paint in the center of it that is about 2 inches in diameter and 1 inch high. Next, place a red blob of paint the same size right on top of the yellow paint. Do not mix them! Lastly, place a blue blob of paint on top of the red blob the same size as the other blobs. You should now have a tower of paint with layers of the three different colors.

1. Which color did you put on your plate first?

   A. Red

   B. Yellow

   C. Blue

2. If the paint represents stratum, which color is oldest?

   A. Red

   B. Yellow

   C. Blue

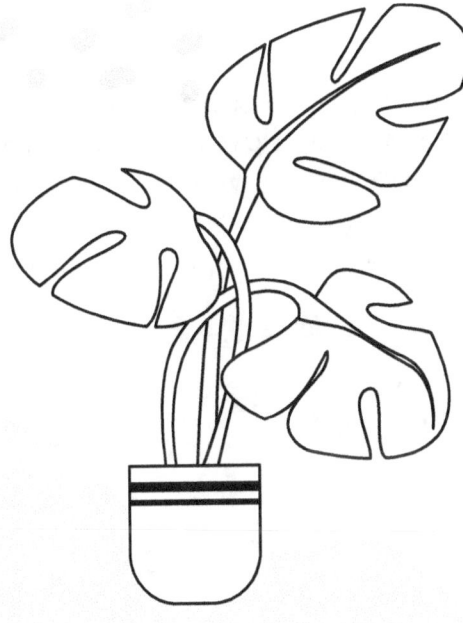

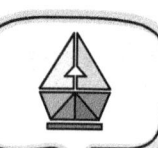
Internet Geology

Find a picture of the Palo Duro Canyon in Amarillo, Texas on the internet and make sure you can see the canyon walls in the picture. Try to count how many layers or stratum you can see.

3. How many different layers did you could in the Palo Duro Canyon?

....

....

....

....

....

Buried In The Sand

Take a shoe box and place a layer of pebble in the bottom of the box. Next place a small plastic figurine in the box and cover it with a layer of sand. Lastly add a layer of potting soil above that.

4. Which layer of stratum is the plastic figurine in?

    A. Pebbles

    B. Sand

    C. Soil

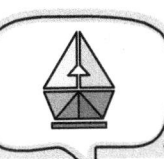
Yesterday, you explored stratum in more detail with three activities. Today you will explain your experience and show how it relates to the topic of the week.

Directions: : Read each text below. Then answer the questions that follow.

Colorful Stratum

You discovered that paint that is put down first represents older stratum and that newer paint is placed on top of it.

1. If the paint represents stratum, which color is the newest layer?

   A. Red

   B. Yellow

   C. Blue

Internet Geology

You discovered that there are lots of different colors of stratum in Palo Duro Canyon.

2. Do you think you could use the stratum at Palo Duro Canyon to figure out the age of a fossil found in them?

   A. Yes

   B. No

3. If there were no stripes on the walls of the canyon, what would that mean?

_____

_____

_____

Buried In The Sand

You discovered that a plastic figurine was found in the middle stratum of sand. This figurine represented a fossil found in a particular layer of Earth's crust.

4. If a different fossil was found in the layer of pebbles in your shoe box, would it be older or newer than the fossil you placed in the layer of sand?

   A. Older

   B. Newer

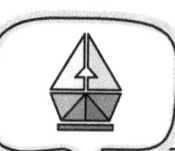
You have spent a few days learning and seeing how stratum is found in layers and that the age of fossils can be determined by what layer of stratum a fossil is found in. Today you will identify the age of fossils based on what stratum they are found in.

Background:

Look at the image found here. This is a cross-section of an archeological dig site in Peru. Archaeologists, a type of scientist that studies fossils, have found lots of different fossils and have also determined the age of each layer of stratum. Look at the image and then answer the questions below.

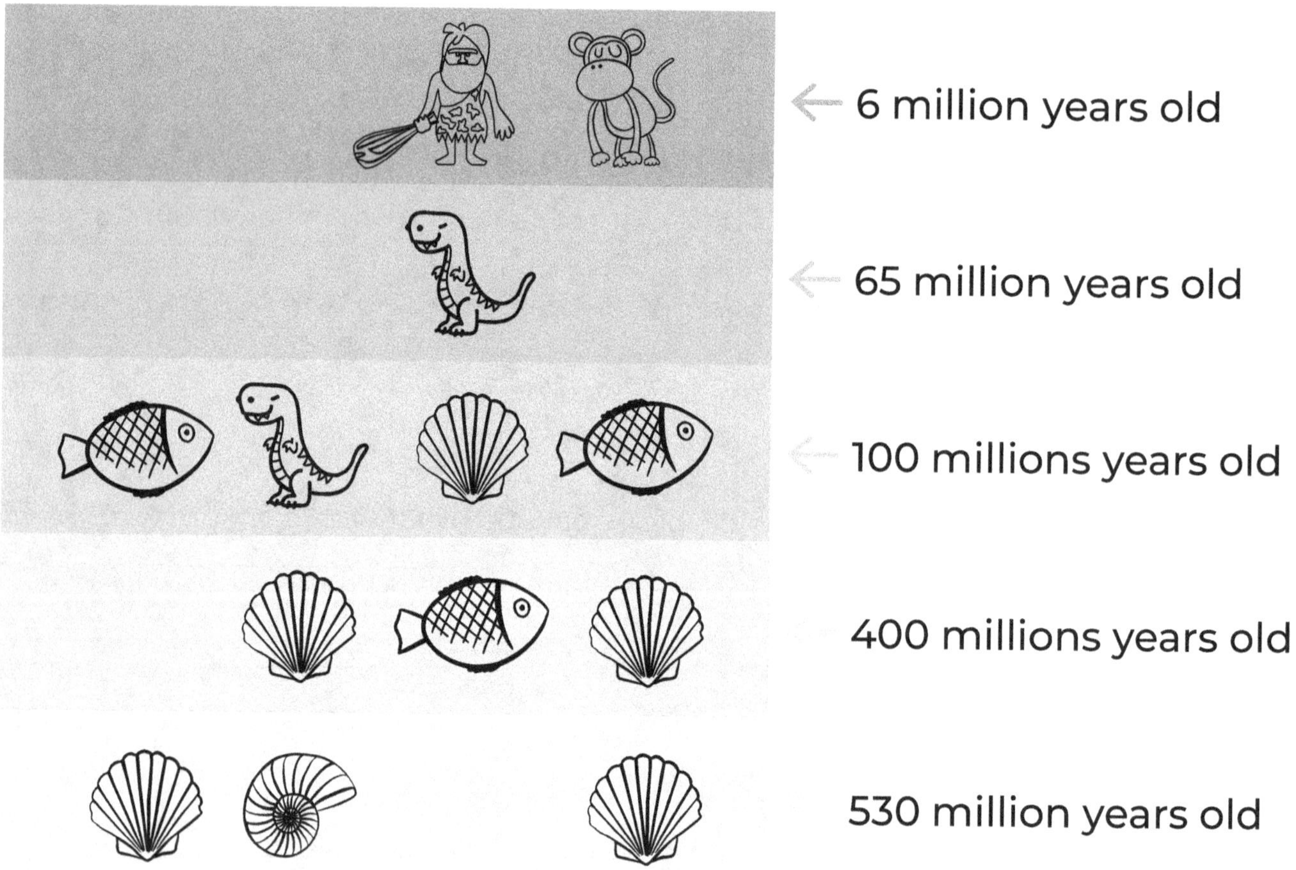

← 6 million years old

← 65 million years old

← 100 millions years old

400 millions years old

530 million years old

Follow-Up Questions:

1. How many different stratum are clams found in?

....

....

2. Which two colors of stratum are dinosaurs found in?

....

....

3. How old are human fossils found at this archaeological site?

....

....

4. What is the range of time that dinosaurs were found on Earth according to the fossils found in stratum?

....

....

....

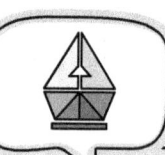
Yesterday, you analyzed an archeological dig site and determined how old different fossils were. Today you will elaborate on your findings just like a real archaeologist would!

Directions: Read and answer each question below.

1. Which animal or animals are the oldest?

2. What color are the layers of stratum that are newer than the stratum that is 100 million years old?

3. Which animals can be found in more than one stratum?

4. Why do you think human and primate (chimpanzee) fossils are only found in the green layer?

5. Why do you think dinosaurs are not found in the green stratum?

WEEK 13

Earth & Space Science

Weathering & Erosion

4-ESS2-1

Make observations and/or measurements to provide evidence of the effects of weathering or the rate of erosion by water, ice, wind, or vegetation.

ARGOPREP

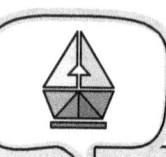
Directions: Read the text below. Then answer the questions that follow.

Changes To Earth's Surface

Go outside on a windy day and notice how the breeze feels on your skin. It probably feels really pleasant. But would you believe that the wind and other types of weather can actually change the surface on our planet? It's true! The process by which wind, rain, and snow alter the shape and size of things like mountains, rivers and canyons is called **weathering**. The main form of weather is called **erosion** which is when rock and soil are worn down over time. This is a very slow process and can take hundreds of thousands of years to occur! Because Earth's surface changes so slowly, you probably won't notice the effects of weathering and erosion in your own lifetime. This week we will focus on weathering and erosion by discussing how they occur and studying how climate change can drastically impact these processes in ways that are not good for the environment.

1. What is it called when wind, rain and snow change the shape of Earth's surface?

   A. Erosion

   B. Canyons

   C. Weathering

   D. Climate change

2. What is it called when rocks and soil are worn down over long periods of time?

   A. Erosion

   B. Canyons

   C. Weathering

   D. Climate change

3. True or false: most of the effects of weathering and erosion can be se~ over our lifetimes.

   A. True

   B. False

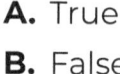

Yesterday, you learned that weathering and erosion can change the surface of Earth. Today you will explore how weathering and erosion work through some fun activities.

Directions: Read each text below and complete the activity. Then answer the questions that follow.

Sugar Mountain

Get a box of sugar cubes and build a mountain that is at least 10 cubes tall. It should be roughly the shape of a pyramid. Now fill a spray bottle with water and then begin to spray the sugar mountain with water. This represents rain. Each time you spray the water bottle, this represents 10 year's worth of rain.

1. Describe how the sugar mountain looks after 10 sprays (100 years)?

_____

_____

_____

2. Describe how the sugar mountain looks after 100 sprays (1000 years)?

_____

_____

_____

Sandbox River

Dig a long, shallow river in the sand of a sandbox. If you do not have a sandbox or there isn't one at a park nearby, you can fill a large plastic box with sand or dirt to do this activity. Pour a few bottles worth of water in one end of the river and watch as the water travels through the channel.

3. As you poured more and more water into the river, did the shape of the river change?

　A. Yes

　B. No

Melting Glaciers

Take an ice cube and place it in the center of a plate. Surround it completely with bread crumbs so that they almost cover the top of it but some of the ice cube is still visible. Wait for the ice cube to melt entirely and then look at the bread crumbs.

4. Did the shape and look of the bread crumbs change after the ice cube melted?

　A. Yes

　B. No

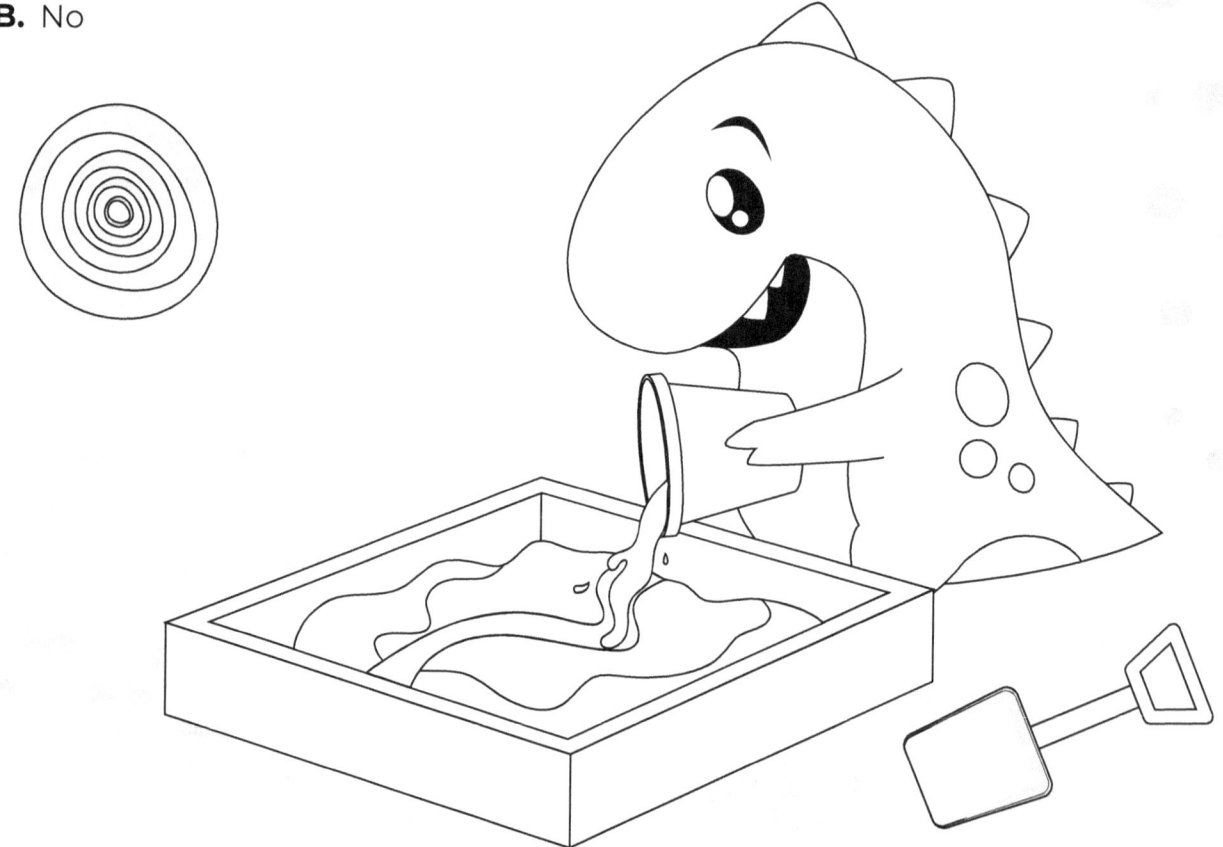

Yesterday, you explored how weathering and erosion work with different activities in your own home. Today you will explain how these processes work based on your observations.

Directions: Read each text below. Then answer the questions that follow.

Sugar Mountain

You discovered spraying water on a mountain made of sugar will change the shape of the mountain over time. The more water is sprayed on it, the more it will change.

1. What does the water coming out of the spray bottle represent?

_____

_____

_____

2. After how many sprays was the mountain most changed?

A. 10

B. 100

Sandbox River

You discovered that as more and more water flowed through your sandbox river, the shape of the riverbed changed.

3. Do you think the Mississippi River, a major river in the United States, looks the same today as it looked 500,000 years ago?

A. Yes

B. No

Melting Glaciers

You discovered that when glaciers melt, they change the land around them.

4. Global climate change is causing the temperatures to increase in areas of the world which are home to large glaciers. How might climate change affect glaciers?

_____

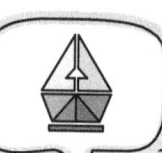
You have spent a few days demonstrating and analyzing the effects of weathering and erosion on Earth's surface. Today you will further explore how global climate change impacts weathering and erosion in different parts of the planet.

Background:

Below is a table that shows three different places on Earth and some information about weathering and erosion in those places. Please read over the table and then answer the questions below. If you are not sure where these places are, feel free to look them up on the Internet.

Place	Temperature Change In The Past 100 Years	Height Of Tallest Mountain In 1800	Height Of Tallest Mountain In 2020	Percent (%) Of Land Lost To Erosion Every Year
Hawaii	4 degrees warmer	13,900 feet	13,800 feet	2%
Kazakhstan	6 degrees warmer	24,500 feet	23,000 feet	1.5%
Australia	5 degrees warmer	8,100 feet	7,300 feet	2.3 %

Follow-Up Questions:

1. What place has increased the most in temperature in the last 100 years?

_____

2. What place has the tallest mountain in 2020?

_____

3. What place had a mountain that was 13,900 feet tall in 1800?

_____

4. Which place is losing about one and a half percent of its land to erosion every year?

_____

5. Which place has the shortest mountain?

_____

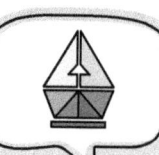
Yesterday, you analyzed data from around the world in order to see how weathering and erosion have changed because of global climate change. Today you will elaborate on this data and draw conclusions about the impacts of climate change.

Directions: Read and answer each question below.

1. What do you notice about the temperatures in all three places?

2. What could have caused all of these mountains to become shorter over time?

3. Do you think climate change affects erosion? Why or why not? Use the data in the table to support your answer.

4. If temperatures around Earth continue to increase, what will also increase?

   A. Weathering

   B. Erosion

   C. All of the above

5. Would it be a good thing or a bad thing for humans if all of our land eroded because of increases in global climate change?

   A. Good

   B. Bad

6. Do you think it is important that we try to stop climate change so that weather and erosion do not change our Earth's surface too quickly?

   A. Yes

   B. No

Earth & Space Science

Earth's Physical Features

4-ESS2-2

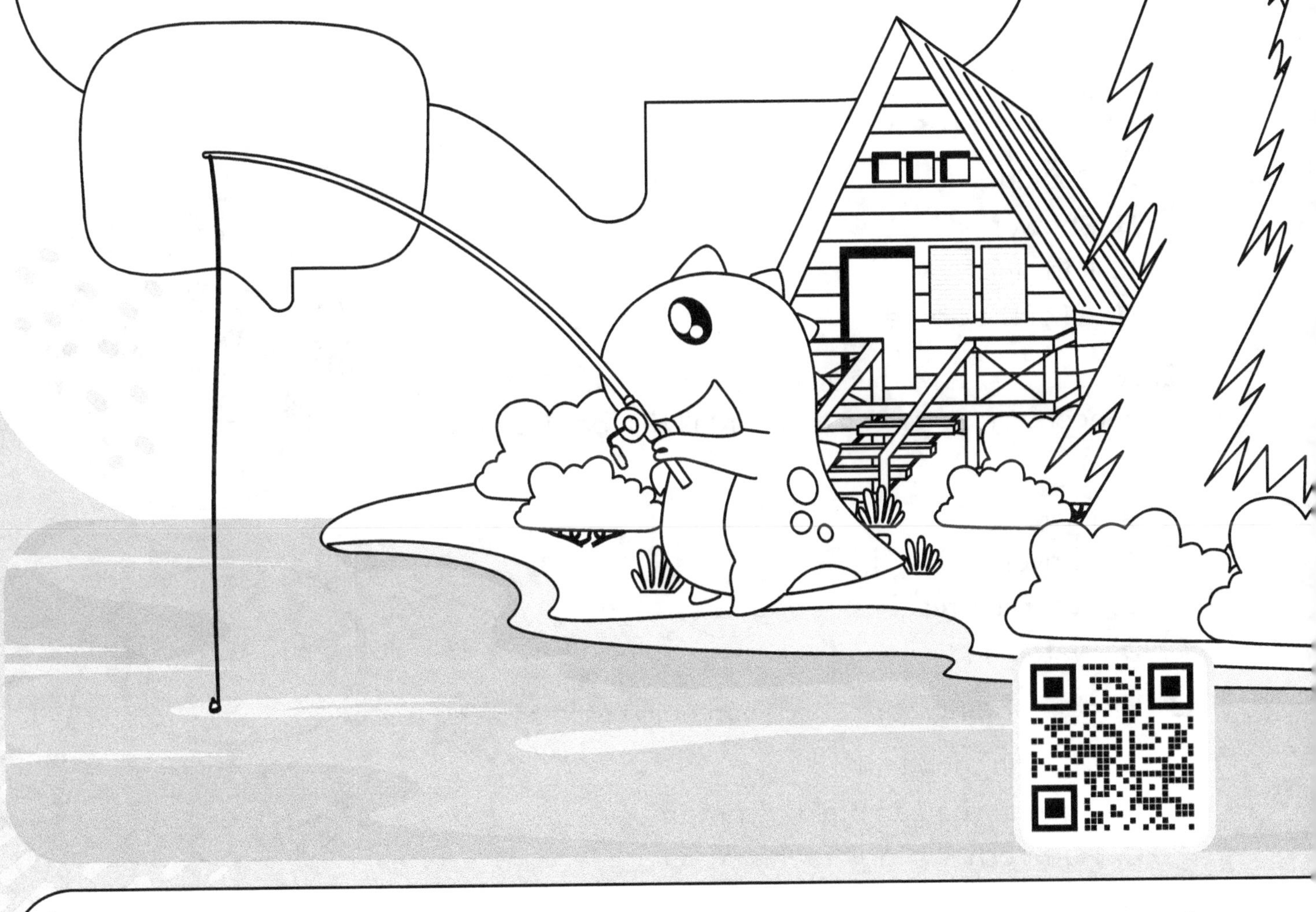

Analyze and interpret data from maps to describe patterns of Earth's features.

ARGOPREP

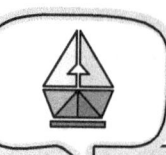
Directions: Read the text below. Then answer the questions that follow.

Exploring Watersheds

Knowing where water collects is very important to us - we use water for everything from farming to cooking to showering and more. Our lives depend on water. Today you will be learning about a major physical feature on Earth called a **watershed**. A watershed is an area that concentrates all of the streams and rainfall to a common outlet such as the mouth of a bay or a large lake. It is very important to understand watersheds because they help us understand where water travels to and can help us decide where to build communities, dams and other important things. Protecting watersheds also helps us protect the environment and all of the other living organisms that rely on water.

1. What do we use water for?

   A. Cooking

   B. Showering

   C. Farming

   D. All of the above

2. A _____ is a physical feature of Earth that concentrates streams and rainfall to a particular area.

   A. Flow

   B. Canyons

   C. Communities

   D. Watershed

3. Understanding watersheds can help us do what?

   A. Change the weather

   B. Decide where to build communities

   C. Harm other living organisms

   D. Take up a lot of our time

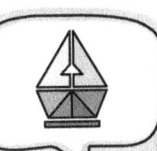
Yesterday, you learned what a watershed is as well as how they are important to living organisms. Today you will explore the physical features of watersheds.

Directions: Read each text below and complete the activity. Then answer the questions that follow.

Which Way Does The Water Go?

Take a bottle of water and pour some of it out. Observe how it moves and where it goes. Now find a small hill and stand at the top of it. Pour the bottle of water onto the ground and notice which way the water travels.

1. When you pour the water out of the bottle, which way does it go?

   A. Up towards the sky

   B. Down towards the ground

2. When you pour water onto the ground at the top of a hill, which way does it travel?

   A. Up the hill

   B. Down the hill

Sandbox Streams

Using a stick, trace a few shallow "streams" into the sand of a sandbox. Make sure they all connect with each other as if they are branches on a tree. If you do not have a sandbox or there isn't one at a park nearby, you can fill a large box with sand or dirt to do this activity. You probably want to pack the dirt down a lot so the water stays in your streams more easily. At one end of one of the streams, pour water and then watch how it travels down and between your other streams.

3. Do you see how water will travel between connected streams?

   A. Yes

   B. No

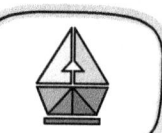
Chesapeake Bay Watershed

Go on the Internet and search for images and pictures of the Chesapeake Bay Watershed. This is a huge watershed on the East Coast of the United States. All of the water that is in this watershed will eventually end up in the Chesapeake Bay which flows into the Atlantic Ocean.

4. What states are part of the Chesapeake Bay Watershed? Choose all that apply.

A. Virginia

B. Maine

C. Delaware

D. Maryland

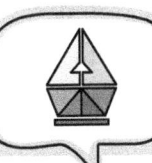
Yesterday, you explored the physical features of watersheds and learned how water travels in and around watersheds. Today you will explain your findings in more detail.

Directions: Read each text below. Then answer the questions that follow.

Which Way Does The Water Go?

You discovered that water always travels down a hill towards the bottom of it.

1. If there are mountains in a watershed and it rains near those mountains, which way will the water eventually flow to?

   A. Down to the bottom of the mountain

   B. Up towards the top of the mountain

Sandbox Streams

You discovered that in a watershed, streams are often connected to each other and water can flow from one stream into others.

2. Go back on the Internet and look up images and pictures of different watersheds around the world. Notice all of the streams and rivers in the images. Do you see how they connect to each other just like the streams you made in the sand yesterday?

   A. Yes

   B. No

Chesapeake Bay Watershed

You discovered that the Chesapeake Bay Watershed is very large and takes up land in a few states.

3. If Maryland started producing a lot of pollution that ended up in their water, what could this do to the whole Chesapeake Bay Watershed? Think about where water ends up in this particular watershed.

_____

_____

_____

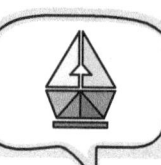
You have spent a few days learning about watersheds. Today you will build your own model of a watershed!

Materials:

1. A tray
2. A thin, plastic shopping bag
3. Scissors
4. 4 cups of different sizes
5. Water
6. Food coloring
7. Pepper

Procedure & Questions:

1. Place your 4 cups on the tray in four different places.
2. Cut down one side of the plastic bag so that you have a flat piece of plastic.
3. Lay the plastic bag over the entire tray and move the plastic so that it touches the tray around the base of the cups.
4. If this is a model of a watershed, what do you think the cups represent?

....

....

....

5. Next, pour some water over the top of one cup and observe where it travels to. Then pour some water over another cup and see where it travels. If you have a hard time seeing the water, add a few cups of food coloring to make it easier to see.

6. Where did the water collect after you poured it over the two different cups?

....

....

....

7. Lastly, sprinkle some pepper on the top of one of the cups. This represents trash and pollution. Then pour water on top of that same cup.

8. Where did the pepper end up after you poured water near it?

....

....

....

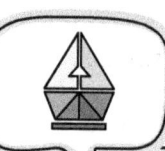

Yesterday, you created a model of a watershed using household materials. Today you will elaborate on your observations and explain how your model shows how an actual watershed would work.

Directions: Read and answer each question below.

1. Are watersheds important?

   A. Yes

   B. No

2. Do you see that water always collects towards the bottom of mountains and at the lowest point in the watershed?

   A. Yes

   B. No

3. Why is it bad to have pollution and trash in a watershed? Think about what happened with the pepper in your model.

   ....

   ....

   ....

4. What could you have added to your model to make it more like a real watershed?

   ....

   ....

   ....

5. If you were going to build a small town in your watershed, where would you place the houses and why?

   ....

   ....

   ....

   ....

Earth & Space Science

Renewable & Nonrenewable Energy

4-ESS3-1

ECO ENERGY

Obtain and combine information to describe that energy and fuels are derived from natural resources and their uses affect the environment.

ARGOPREP

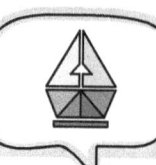
Directions: Read the text below. Then answer the questions that follow.

Different Types Of Energy

Think about all of the things that use power in your life - televisions, computers, cars, stoves, washing machines and so much more. Energy comes in many different forms in our home including heat and electricity. But did you know that there are different places where energy comes from?

Energy can be broken down into two categories: renewable and nonrenewable energy. **Renewable energy** comes from things like wind, water and the sun. This energy is renewable because we will never run out of these types of energy. **Nonrenewable energy** comes from things like coal, natural gas, oil and nuclear substances. This energy is renewable because one day, perhaps very soon, we will use all of it up and won't be able to make more of it. Some nonrenewable energy also has the drawback of being bad for the environment.

1. What is needed in order to use a washing machine, cell phone, computer and a car?

A. Water

B. Driver's license

C. Energy

D. The sun

2. Power from the sun, wind and water is called .... energy.

A. Heat

B. Renewable energy

C. Coal

D. Nonrenewable energy

3. What is one drawback to nonrenewable energy?

A. It is bad for the environment

B. We have lots of it on Earth

C. It smells weird

D. It can't be used to power a car

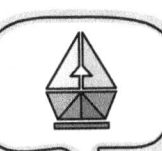
Yesterday, you learned about the difference between renewable and nonrenewable energy. Today you will explore these types of energy in more detail.

Directions: Read each text below and complete the activity. Then answer the questions that follow.

Nonrenewable Energy

Oil and coal are called **fossil fuels** because they are created when fossils are stuck in the ground for millions of years. The pressure and heat of being underground turns fossils into coal and oil. When we burn coal and oil to make energy, it releases a lot of carbon dioxide into the environment and causes our planet to get hotter and more polluted.

1. Do you see that it takes a very long time to make fossil fuels?

    A. Yes

    B. No

2. What is released into the environment when you burn coal and oil?

    A. Oxygen

    B. Carbon dioxide

    C. Fossil fuels

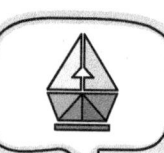
Renewable Energy: Solar Power

Stand in the sunlight on a bright day. Do you notice how warm it feels? The sunlight that comes from the sun has a lot of energy which can be captured with **solar panels** and turned into heat and electricity. The Sun will be around for a very long time so we can continue to get energy from it, making it a renewable energy source.

3. What types of energy can sunlight be turned into?

....

....

Renewable Energy: Hydropower

As you saw last week in your lessons about watersheds, water is always moving and flowing from one place to another. The movement of water can be used to turn **turbines**. Turbines look like large wheels and when they turn, they make electricity. Since we have lots of moving water on Earth, we can make hydropower (power that comes from water) for as long as we want.

4. What is the name of the thing that can turn the movement of water into electricity?

....

....

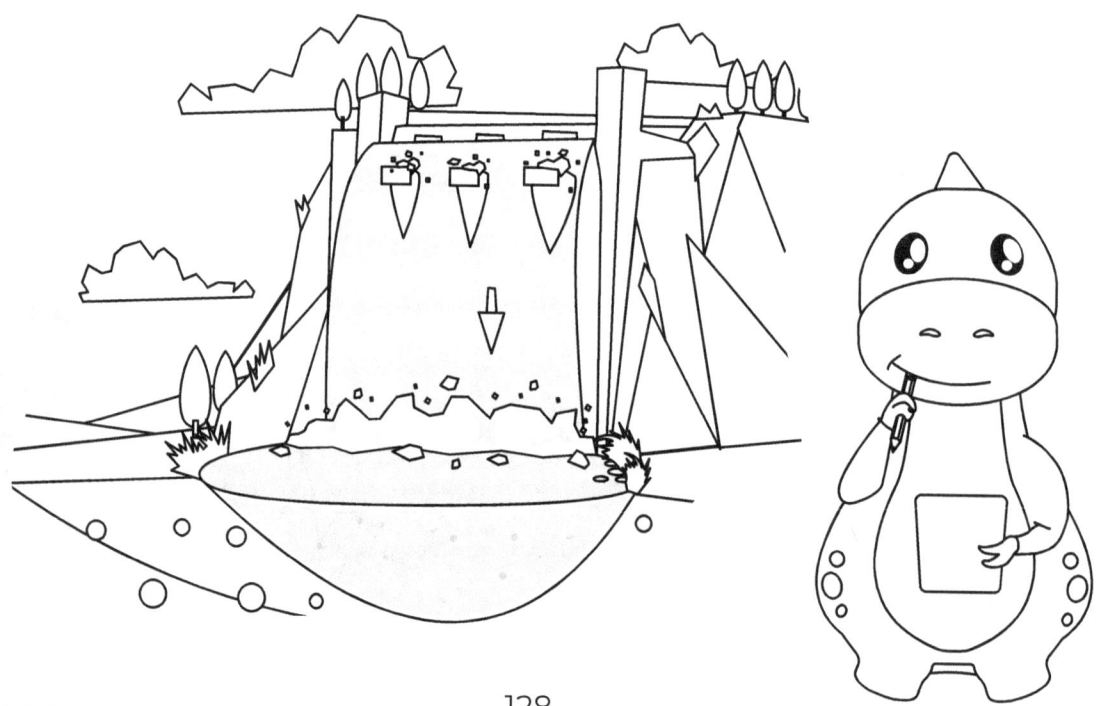

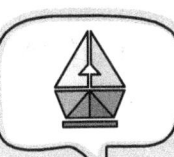
Yesterday, you explored different types of renewable and nonrenewable energy. Today you will explain how they work in a bit more detail.

Directions: Read each text below. Then answer the questions that follow.

Nonrenewable Energy

You discovered that it takes a long time for fossil fuels to be made and that they can pollute the environment when we use them to make energy.

1. Do you think we should use fossil fuels to make energy? Why or why not?

....

....

....

....

Renewable Energy: Solar Power

You discovered that solar power can be used to make heat and electricity. You also learned that there we will always have access to sunlight.

2. You learned yesterday that we capture the sun's energy with solar panels. Do some research on the Internet and list 3 places on Earth that would be a great place to put solar panels. You want to look for places that get a lot of sunlight.

....

....

....

....

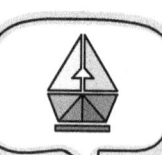
Renewable Energy: Hydropower

You discovered moving water turns turbines which then make energy. You also learned that there is lots of flowing water on our planet so this resource will never run out.

3. Where near your home would be a good place for you to put turbines? Think about a major river or dam that is close to your home. You can research this online or ask a parent for help if you need it.

....
....
....
....
....
....
....

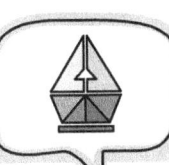
You have spent a few days learning about the differences between renewable and nonrenewable energy. Today you will spend some time today tracking all of the way you use electricity and other forms of energy throughout the day.

Background:

Similar to hydropower, wind power is captured with wind turbines. Wind turbines look like large pinwheels that can be up to 20 stories tall! Wind turns the blades of the wind turbine which creates electricity that can be used to power entire towns and cities. Start today by looking at images and videos of wind turbines online.

Procedure:

Answer the questions below as you go throughout your day today in order to determine all of the ways you use energy in your home.

Follow-Up Questions:

1. List 3 things in your kitchen that use electricity.

....

....

....

2. How many electric lamps or lights do you have in your home?

....

....

3. How do you heat your home when it is cold?

....

....

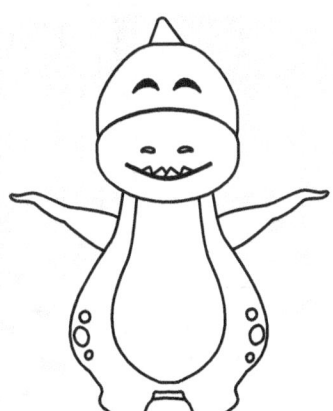

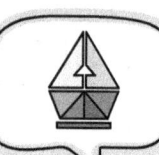
4. Do you or your family members have cell phones?

A. How often do cell phones need to be charged?

5. Do you need to use electricity to wash your clothes?

A. Do you dry your clothes in a dryer or hang them up on a laundry line?

6. What kind of energy does your car use? If your family does not have a car, how do they get around and does it require energy?

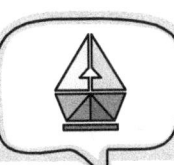
Yesterday, you looked at all the ways you use energy in your own home. Today you will elaborate on this information by thinking about what types of energy you should power your home with.

Directions: Read and answer each question below.

1. What do you think you spend the most amount of energy on every day in your home?

....

....

....

2. Why do you think it is better to use renewable energy instead of nonrenewable energy?

....

....

....

3. Think about where you live: would it be easier to power your home with solar energy or with hydropower?

....

....

....

4. Do you think wind turbines are a good form of energy to have in a big city? Why or why not?

....

....

....

5. Can we make more nonrenewable energy sources if we run out of them?

    A. Yes

    B. No

WEEK 16

Earth & Space Science

Human Impact On Earth

4-ESS3-2

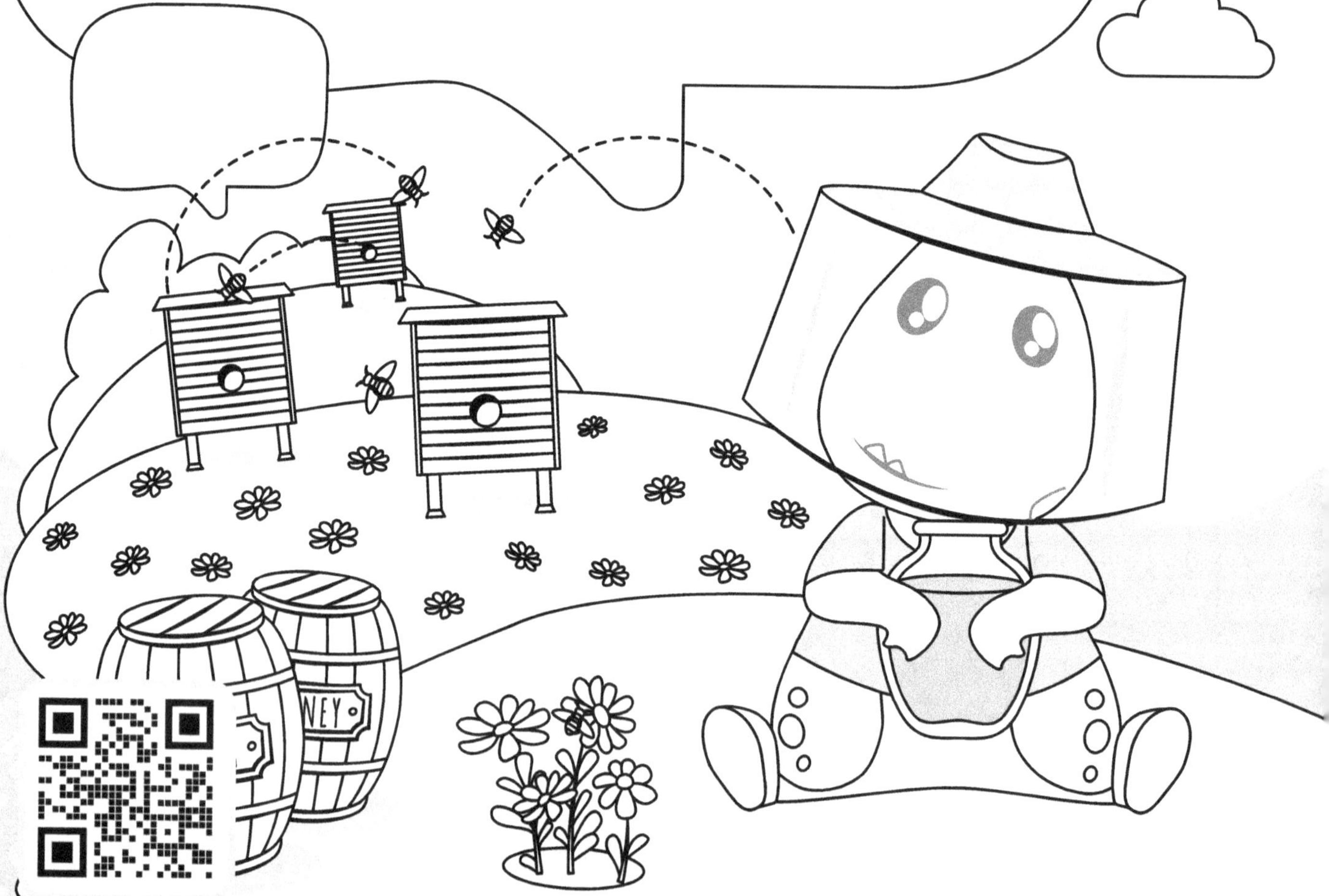

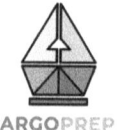

Generate and compare multiple solutions to reduce the impacts of natural Earth processes on humans.

ARGOPREP

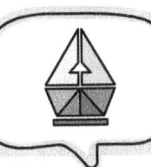
Directions: Read the text below. Then answer the questions that follow.

Our Planet, Our Impact

As you have seen since you began this workbook, we interact with our environment every day. Our habits impact plants and animals, we use land in order to grow food, we build houses which take up space and so much more. Many of our behaviors, however, impact the world in negative ways. For example, you've heard about global **climate change** in previous lessons in this workbook. We have created pollution and changes to the world that are changing the temperatures on our planet and causing harm to other living creatures. **Deforestation** occurs when humans cut down lots of trees to make room for other things like buildings and roads. The human **population**, the number of humans on the planet, is growing at such a quick rate that it can be hard to provide resources like food and shelter for everyone on Earth. This week we will explore how humans impact the Earth and how you can help to protect the planet!

1. What is it called when humans cut down lots of trees to make room for other things?

   A. Climate change

   B. Deforestation

   C. Impact

   D. Population

2. What is one cause of climate change?

   A. Heat

   B. Growth

   C. Pollution

   D. Plants

3. What is happening now that the human population is growing very fast and getting very big?

   A. We have more resources

   B. We have less resources

   C. We are planting more trees

   D. Nothing has changed

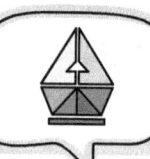
Yesterday, you learned that humans can negatively impact the environment in a number of different ways. Today you will explore this impact with a few activities around your own home.

Directions: Read each text below and complete the activity. Then answer the questions that follow.

Green Spaces & Buildings

Ask your parents to take a walk with you around a local park. Then go to an area in your town or city that has lots of buildings and businesses. If you live far away from an area like this, go online and look up pictures of Manhattan to get a sense of a busy city.

1. Do you notice more plants and animals at the park or in the area with buildings and businesses?

....

....

2. If there had been a forest of trees in a city a long time ago, what would humans have had to do in order to make room for buildings?

   A. Climate change

   B. Deforestation

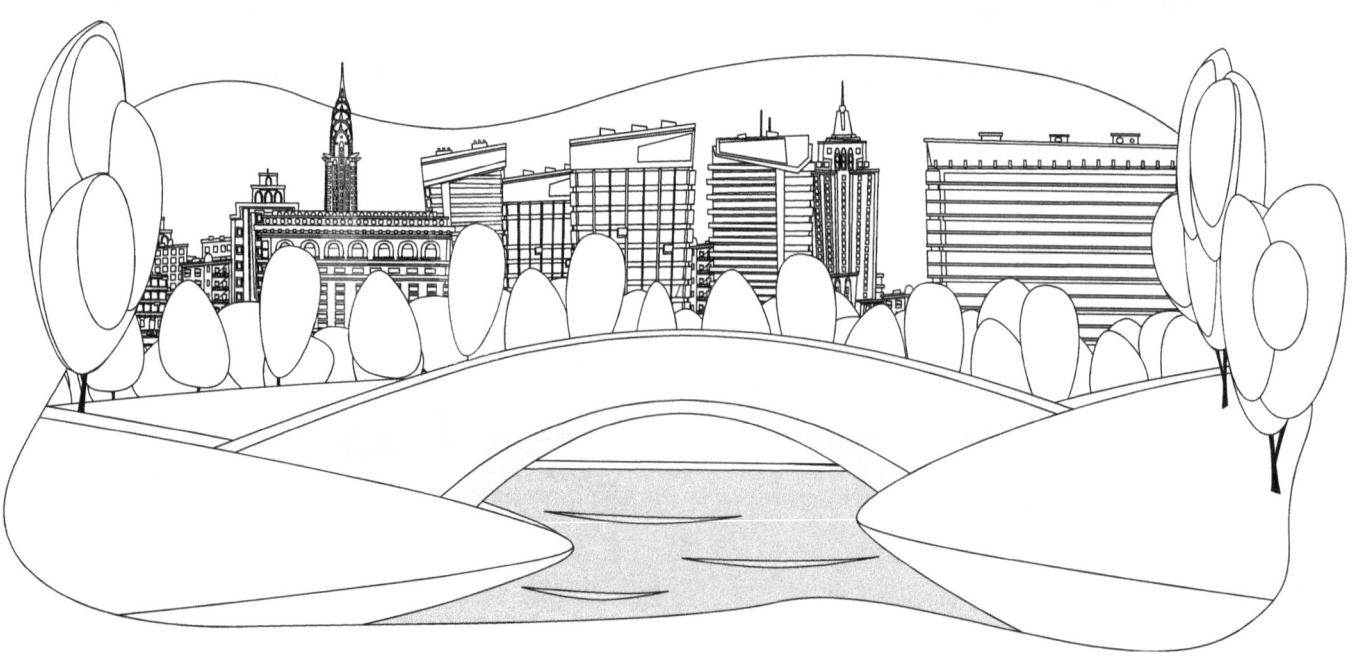

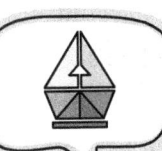
Bicycles Vs. Cars

Most cars are powered by gas - in a previous lesson you learned that when gas, a fossil fuel, is burned, it releases carbon dioxide into the air. Carbon dioxide is a form of pollution.

3. If you are riding a bicycle, do you create any pollution?

....

....

....

....

Resources We All Need

Take a moment to consider what you and your family need in order to live. You need water, food, and shelter. Those are necessary. You also need transportation, money, education and lots of other things. Make a list of all of the things you use in one single day.

4. Do you see that humans require a lot of resources in order to survive?

   A. Yes
   B. No

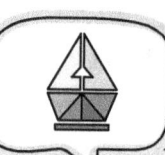
Yesterday, you explored how you and your home impact the environment around you. Today you will explain what that impact is and how we can all work towards making things better for Earth.

Directions: Read each text below. Then answer the questions that follow.

Green Spaces & Buildings

You discovered that when we create buildings and businesses, we take away space from plants and animals.

1. What is one thing we could do to help plants and animals when we take up their space with buildings? You can do some research online if it helps you brainstorm an idea.

_____

_____

_____

_____

_____

Bicycles Vs. Cars

You discovered that gas cars add to pollution in the air whereas riding a bicycle does not.

2. What does pollution from cars lead to?

    A. Overpopulation

    B. Deforestation

    C. Climate change

3. Do you think people should try to drive more or use their bicycles more if they want to save the planet?

_____

_____

_____

_____

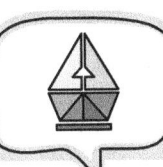

Resources We All Need

You discovered that people need a lot of resources every day.

4. What is one resource you absolutely cannot live without? Think about resources that help you survive.

....

....

....

....

....

....

5. If there is a set amount of resources on this planet, but there are more and more people, are there going to be more resources for each person or less resources for each person?

A. More resource for each person

B. Less resources for each person

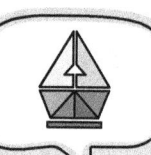
You have spent a few days learning about how different human activities impact the planet. Today you will build a model of a green space you could build in your own community to provide space and resources for local plants and animals.

Materials:

1. Computer with the internet
2. Colored construction paper
3. Colored pencils or markers
4. Recycles cardboard
5. Glue and/or tape
6. Crafting materials like beads, felt, popsicle sticks or whatever else you have laying around your home

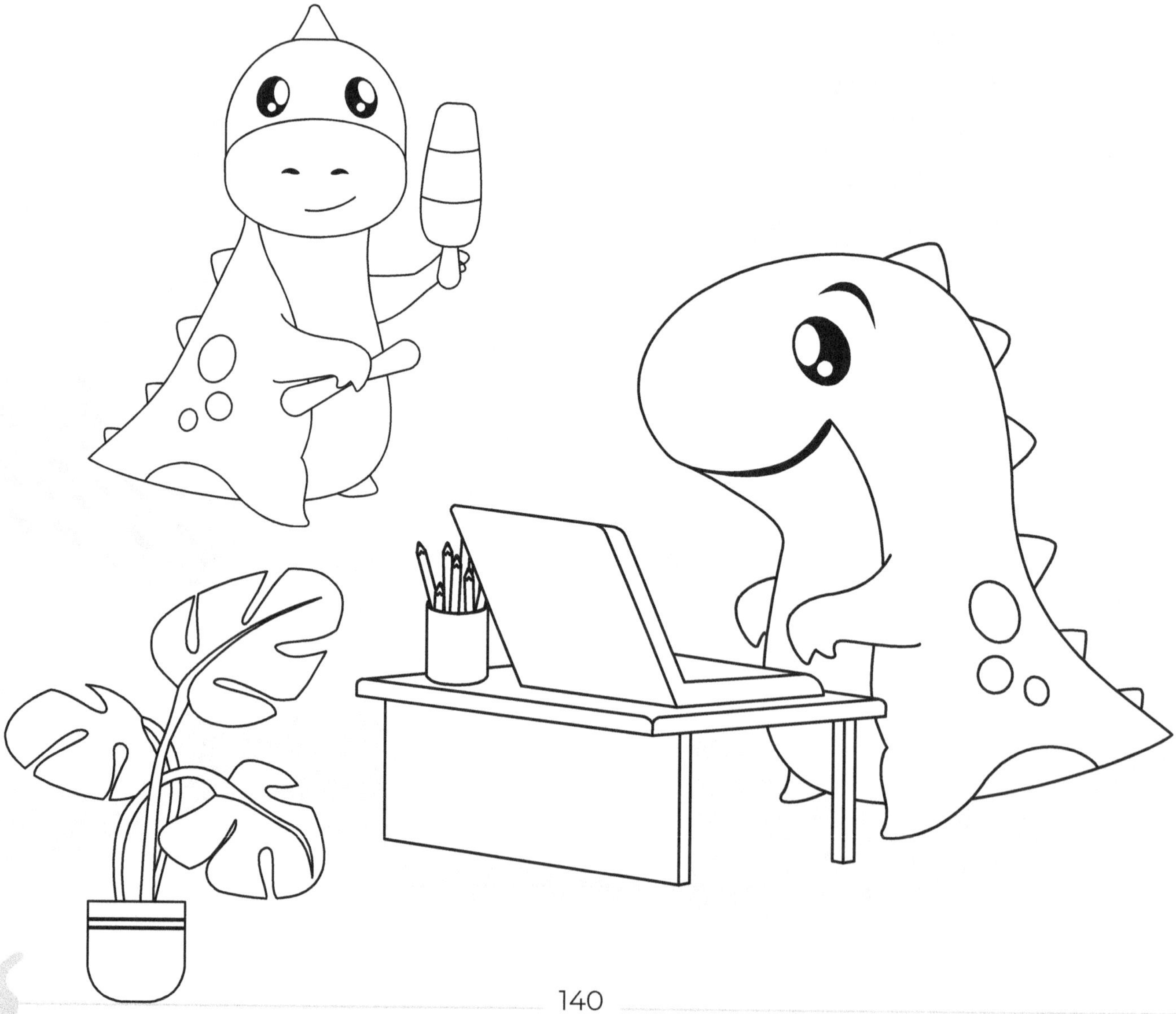

Procedure:

1. Start by going online and researching "green spaces" "habitats" and community gardens on the Internet. Think about what these types of spaces are and how they help plants and animals.

2. On a piece of paper, draw out a green space that you could imagine creating in your own community. Think about different things you'd want to have in order to help plants and animals. These things could include (but are not limited to):

   A. Bird houses

   B. A butterfly garden with flowers that butterflies feed of of

   C. An apiary (a home for bees)

   D. Vegetable garden

   E. Wildflower meadow

   F. Pond for fish and amphibians

3. Once you have your design drawn, make a 3-D model of it using construction paper, cardboard, and any other crafting materials you have access to. Make it colorful and fun! Add labels so whoever is looking at your model knows what all of the different exciting things are in your green space.

4. Show your amazing model to your friends and family. Ask them what they like about it and what they might add so that you can help plants and animals have a home in the environment.

5. Feel free to add or change your model as you go in case you think of something else that could be helpful. For example, maybe you decide as you are working on your model that you will add a bench so people can sit and look at all the plants and animals enjoying your beautiful green space.

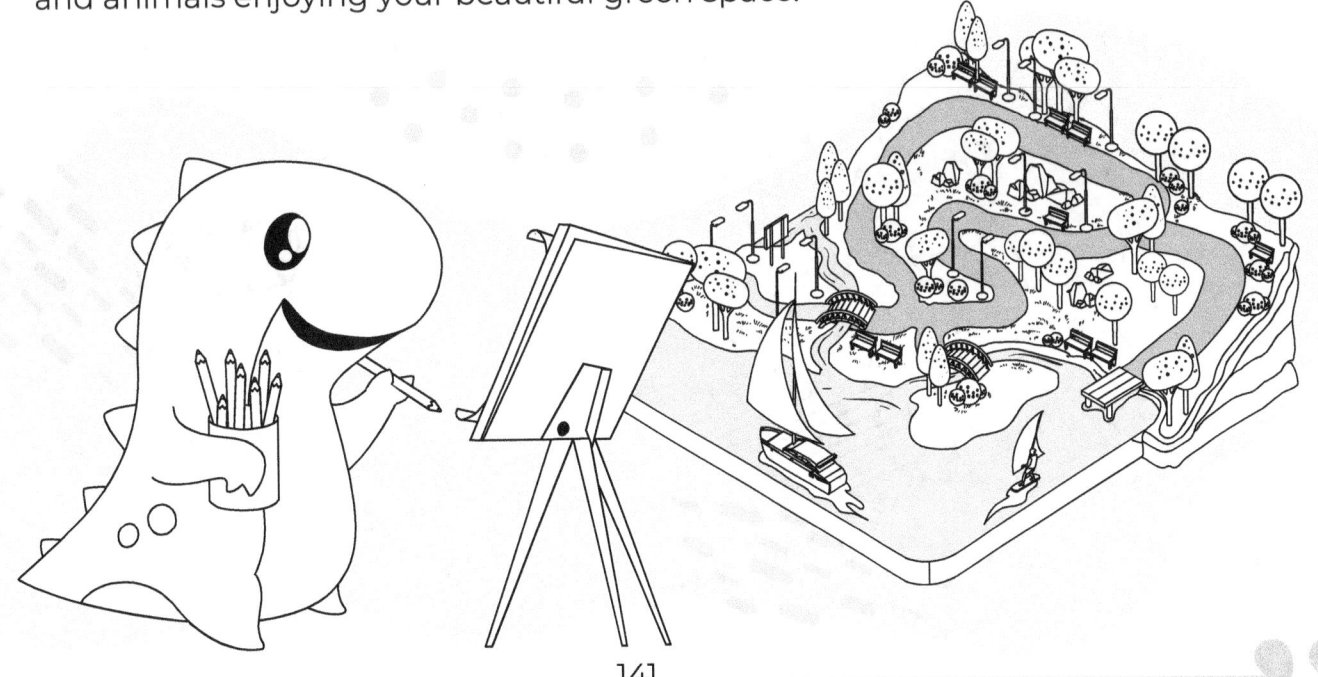

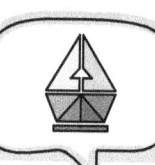
Yesterday, you designed and built a 3-D model of a green space that you would love to have in your own community. Today you will elaborate on why you made certain choices with your model and how they help the environment.

Directions: Read and answer each question below.

1. What is your favorite part of your model and why?

2. How does the part of the green space you chose for question #1 help plants or animals?

3. If you could add one additional thing to your model, what would you choose?

4. What is one thing you could add to a green space to help the human population and why?

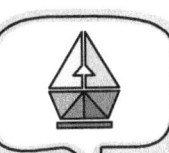
5. What is one thing you could add to a green space to help people minimize pollution?

....

....

6. What is one thing you could do with your green space that would help with the negative effects of deforestation?

....

....

7. Do you think it is important to help the planet and make sure we don't harm it with our human impact?

....

....

....

Engineering
Defining Design Problems

3-5-ETS1-1

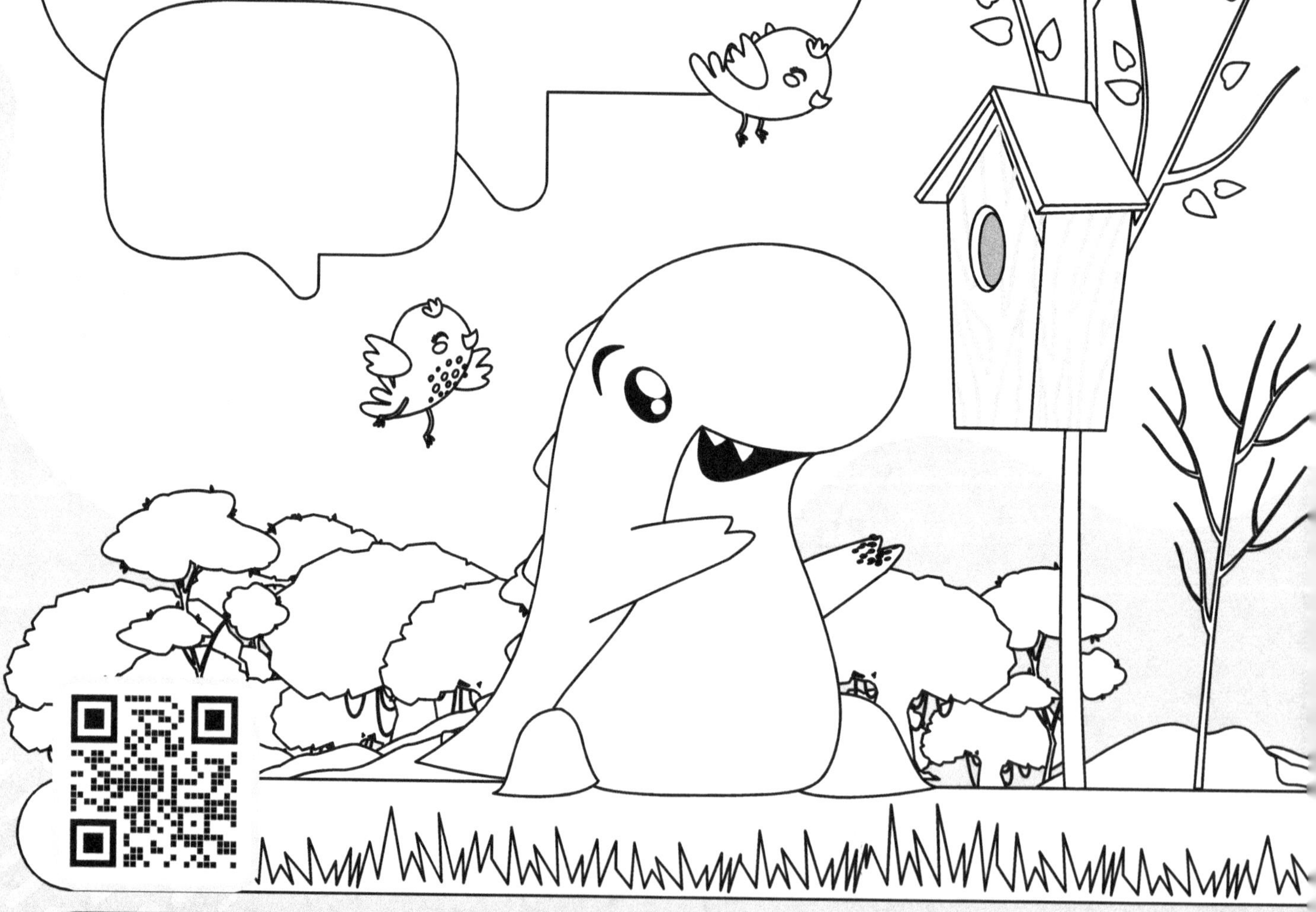

Define a simple design problem reflecting a need or a want.

ARGOPREP

Directions: Read the text below. Then answer the questions that follow.

What Is A Design Problem?

Engineers are a type of scientist whose job it is to improve the design of things. Think about it - have you ever had a toy or a belonging which you liked but could maybe be improved some way? Chances are that you have. This week we are going to practice identifying **design problems** so that in future lessons you can become an engineer and fix these problems so that the design of something is even better! Here is an example: pretend you have a chair in your room that you sit in to do homework and read. You like the color of the chair and the material it is made out of, but it is a bit too tall for you and your legs can't reach the ground when you sit in it. This makes it uncomfortable for you. The design problem of this chair is that the chair is too tall.

1. What types of scientists focus on improving the design of things?

   A. Biologist

   B. Chemists

   C. Naturalists

   D. Engineers

2. When something is not perfect, what is the issue called that an engineer will try to fix?

   A. A solution

   B. A design problem

   C. Results

   D. Color

3. Do you think it is important to try to improve objects so that their design is better?

   A. Yes

   B. No

   C. Unsure

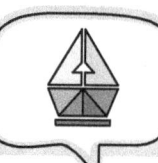
Yesterday, you learned that part of an engineers job is to figure out design problems. Today you will explore this idea by practicing identifying design problems around your home.

Directions: Read each text below and complete the activity. Then answer the questions that follow.

Kitchen Counters

Go stand in your kitchen and notice the height of the kitchen counters. If you were mixing something in a bowl on the countertop, would it be the right height for you? Is it too tall, too short, or just the right height?

1. What might be the design problem if you are somewhat short?

_____

_____

_____

2. Is there a design problem if the counter is the right height for you and you can use it comfortably?

_____

_____

_____

Stale Bread

You notice that the package that a loaf of bread comes in is hard to close once it has been opened. It doesn't stay shut even when you use a twist tie to try to close it. As a result the bread gets stale very quickly and is no longer tasty when you eat it.

3. What is the design problem in this example?

....

....

....

....

Big & Little Seeds

You buy a bag of bird seed and notice that all of the seeds in the bag are very lage. The seeds in this bird seed mix are sunflower seeds, acorns and walnuts. You notice that when you put it in your bird feeder, the birds with large beaks can eat the seeds but smaller birds cannot. The small bird's beaks seem to be too small to crack the very large seeds.

4. Is there a design problem with the mix of seeds in your bird seed?

   A. Yes

   B. No

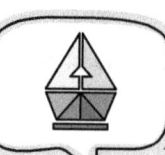
Yesterday, you explored different design problems in various examples. Today you will elaborate on those design problems and think about how you might fix them.

Directions: Read each text below. Then answer the questions that follow.

Kitchen Counters

You discovered that your kitchen counters are the right height if a person is a certain height.

1. If a person is very short, how could you improve the design of the countertops so that it is easier for them to use them comfortably?

....

....

....

....

....

Stale Bread

You discovered that there is a design problem with the bread bag which leads the bread to become very stale quickly.

2. Think of and describe one way you could fix the design problem of a bread bag that is hard to keep closed.

....

....

....

....

....

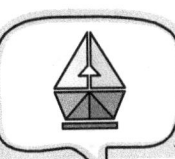
Big & Little Seeds

You discovered that the mix of bird seed in this example has very big seeds in it which larger birds with large beaks can eat easily.

3. What is the design problem with the mix of bird seed?

....

....

....

....

4. How could you fix the design problem with the bird seed?

....

....

....

....

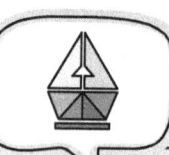
You have spent a few days practicing how to identify a design problem. Today you will pick something in your home that needs improvement and try to identify what the design problem is with this object.

Materials:

1. One object of your choosing in your home (such as a toy, a piece of clothing, a small piece of furniture, etc)

Procedure & Questions:

1. Identify what object you are going to work with for this lesson. Make sure it is in front of you.

....

....

2. Now you are going to be an engineer! Start by writing down all of the different attributes you can see that are part of your object. Just look, don't touch it. This could include things like color, shape, height, and the materials it is made out of. List them below.

....

....

....

....

....

3. Now touch your object. If it is small you can move it around in your hands. If it is larger or heavier, move around it and touch it in different places. If it is furniture, you could even sit on it! List all the things you notice when you touch it. These include its temperature, texture, or weight.

....

....

....

4. Now think about this object and how it is used. Is there anything you do not like about the design of this object? Or maybe you like everything about it, but is there a way it could be made even better? Below, list three things that you think are **design problems** with this object.

....

....

....

5. Lastly, for each of the three things you listed for question #4, write one sentence that explains <u>why</u> you think it is a design problem.

....

....

....

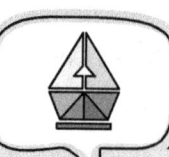
Yesterday, you chose an object in your house and identified some design problems with it. Today you will elaborate on the design problems and choose one that you will focus on fixing.

Directions: Read and answer each question below.

1. Do you think your object could be improved by an engineer in some way?

    A. Yes

    B. No

2. Which design problem is most important to you and why?

3. What are three solutions you can think of to improve your design problem?

4. Which of the solutions are ones that you think you could easily do yourself?

5. Do you think engineers are important?

6. If we did not have engineers, what do you think would happen?

WEEK 18

Engineering
Design Constraints

3-5-ETS1-1

Define a simple design problem reflecting a need or a want that includes specified criteria for success and constraints on materials, time, or cost.

ARGOPREP

Directions: Read the text below. Then answer the questions that follow.

Limits & Design Problems

After an engineer has identified a design problem, they need to find a solution to that problem. But not all solutions are always possible. For example, let's say you are designing a box and want it to be very strong. You have $10 to use towards your design. You cannot make your box out of solid silver metal, however, because that would cost much more than $10. You can see how your budget of $10 **limits** the solutions you can choose for your design. Other limits could include time, space, or materials available. When you have limits on the solutions you can choose to fix a design problem, it is not always a bad thing. It just means you need to think creatively about how to solve the problem! If you work hard enough you can find a solution even if you have lots of limits.

1. Are all solutions to a problem possible if you have a limit?

    A. Yes

    B. No

2. Which of the following is NOT a design limit?

    A. A solution

    B. Budget

    C. Time

    D. Material availability

3. If you had only 20 minutes to solve a problem, what design limit do you have?

    A. Time

    B. Budget

    C. Space

    D. Material availability

Yesterday, you learned that there can sometimes be limits to solutions you come up with to a design problem. Today you will explore identifying solutions when you have various limits.

Directions: Read each text below and complete the activity. Then answer the questions that follow.

Space

Tracy needs to fit all of her clothing into one dresser in her room. The space she has in her room is 3 feet wide by 4 feet tall for the dresser. She goes to the store to shop for dressers. Which of the following dressers would be the best choice based on the limit of space she has in her room?

4 feet wide by 3 feet tall

3 feet wide by 3 feet tall

2 feet wide by 5 feet tall

Budget

Manhu is cooking a delicious dinner for himself and four of his best friends. He wants to make sure the ingredients cost him less than $22 dollars. Below is a list of ingredients he needs for his meal and their prices.

- Chicken $8
- Spinach $3
- Pasta $3
- Sauce $5
- Cheese $4

1. Did Manhu choose ingredients which are within his budget?

A. Yes

B. No

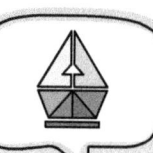
Materials

Grace is designing a birdbath for her grandfather's garden. She wants to make sure it can hold a small amount of water for the birds. She also wants to make sure it is sturdy. She only has access to the following materials: Concrete, wood, and cardboard.

2. Which material would not be a good choice for Grace to design and make her bird bath from?

    A. Concrete

    B. Wood

    C. Cardboard

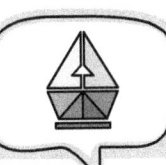
Yesterday, you explored different design problems in various examples. Today you will elaborate on those design problems and think about how you might fix them.

Directions: Read each text below. Then answer the questions that follow.

Space

You discovered that not all of the dressers at the store fit Tracy's design limits in terms of space.

1. Why would a dresser that is 2 feet wide and 5 feet tall not be a good choice for Tracy?

_____

_____

_____

_____

_____

_____

Budget

You discovered that Madhu chose ingredients that added up to more than his budget for the meal he is cooking for his friends.

2. What is something Madhu could do in order to make sure he is within his budget for his meal?

_____

_____

_____

_____

_____

_____

Materials

You discovered that Grace should not choose to make a birdbath out of cardboard.

3. Why would cardboard not be the best choice choice for a material to use?

....

....

....

....

4. Which other material, wood or concrete, would you prefer to make a birdbath out of and why?

....

....

....

....

....

You have spent a few days practicing how to identify solutions to a design problem that are within your limits. Today you will go back to the design problems you thought about last week in regards to an object in your house. Today you will think about how you would solve these problems under certain limits.

Materials:

1. Same object of your choosing in your home that you worked with last week

Procedure & Questions:

1. Start by looking back at the design problem you focused on last week during day #5. Restate that design problem below:

....

....

....

2. Now choose one of your three solutions to that problem that you came up with that day. Restate that solution below:

....

....

....

....

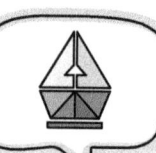
3. In the space below draw a picture of what you want your object to look like with your design solution.

4. Do some research and determine how much it would cost you to redesign your object with at that particular solution: Write your budget for your solution below:

....

....

....

5. If you had a limit of only 1 hour to complete this solution, do you think you could do it?

A. Yes

B. No

6. If you only had access to cardboard and construction paper, would you be able to use your solution for this design problem? Or would the materials limit you?

....

....

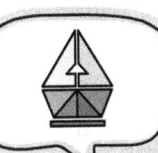
Yesterday, you considered how you might redesign an object in your house if you had different limits. Today you will elaborate on this process.

Directions: Read and answer each question below.

1. Could you choose your solution to your design problem if you had a budget of $10?

2. If you had a whole month to complete your design, do you think you could use the solution you initially chose?

3. What materials do you need to have access to in order to complete your design in the way you want to?

4. Do you see how limits can change how you design an object?

   A. Yes

   B. No

5. Do you see how being creative can help you overcome limits?

   A. Yes

   B. No

Engineering
Comparing Solutions

3-5-ETS1-2

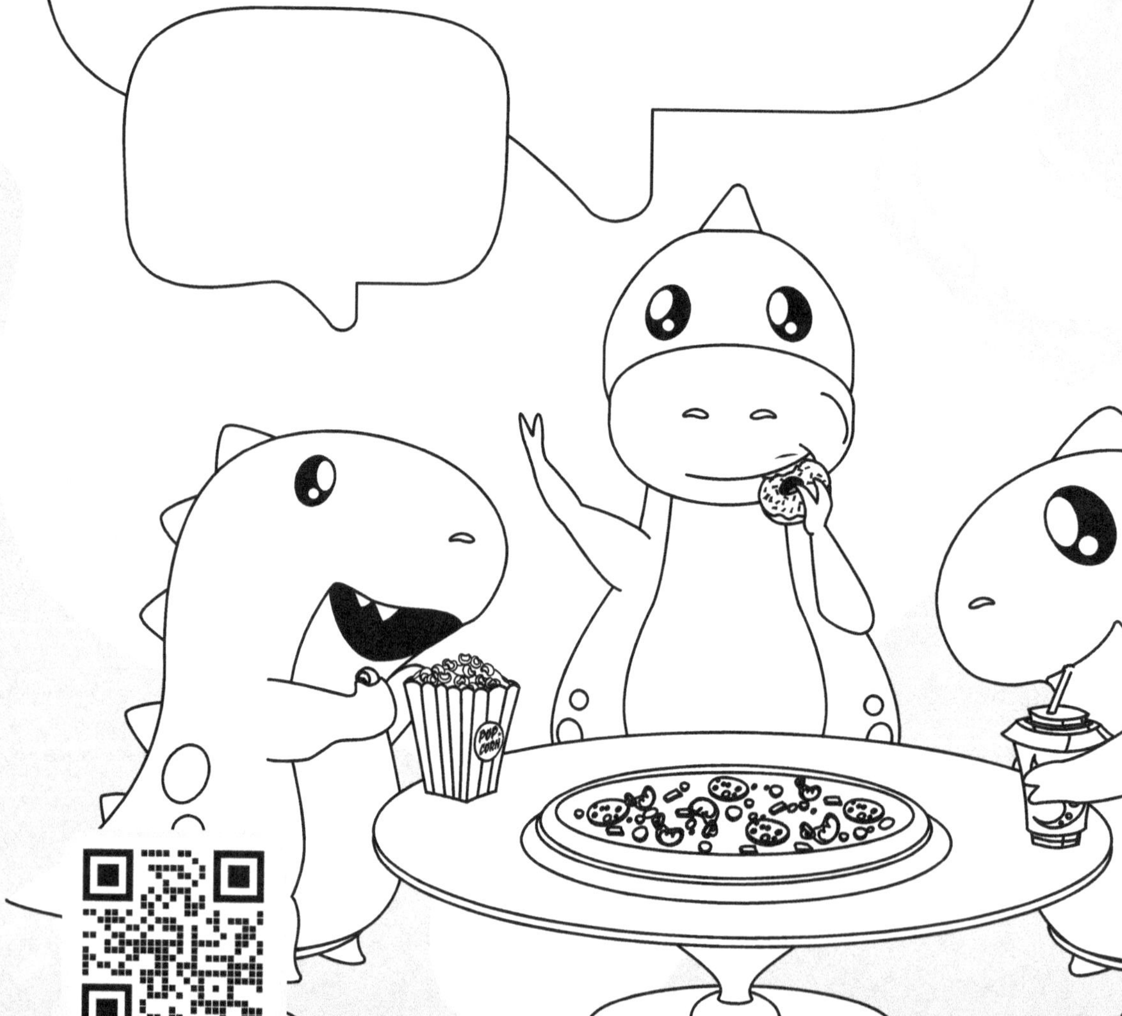

Generate and compare multiple possible solutions to a problem based on how well each is likely to meet the criteria and constraints of the problem.

ARGOPREP

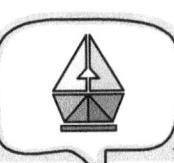
Directions: Read the text below. Then answer the questions that follow.

Which Solution Is The Best One?

As you can see from the previous weeks of lessons, sometimes there is more than one solution to a problem. For example, if you wanted to make a sofa more comfortable, you could do a few things. You could cover it in softer fabric or add more pillows. But which solution is better? Oftentimes, scientists and engineers will **test** their ideas before choosing to go with one solution. When they conduct a test, they get **results**. Results are a kind of information which can be used to figure out which solution is the best one. Let's say you wanted to test out your solutions for your sofa - you ask 10 people to sit on a sofa that is bigger as well as one that is covered in a softer fabric. If 8 of those 10 people say the softer sofa is more comfortable, you know that is the best solution to your problem. Today you will practice testing solutions and choosing the best one.

1. Can there be more than one good solution to a problem?

    A. Yes

    B. No

2. How can you decide which solution to use?

    A. By doing nothing

    B. By coming up with more ideas

    C. By testing your ideas

    D. By forgetting about the problem

3. What do scientists get when they complete a test that they can then use to choose a solution?

    A. More solutions

    B. Other tests

    C. Confusion

    D. Results

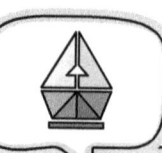
Yesterday, you learned that in order to choose the best solution to a design problem, you want to conduct a test and get some results. Today you will analyze some tests and determine what their results mean.

Directions: Read each text below and complete the activity. Then answer the questions that follow.

Favorite Nuts

Agustus wants to start providing food for the neighborhood squirrels but he does not know if they prefer walnuts or peanuts. He places a handful out on his porch every day for a whole week. Every day he finds that the squirrels eat the whole pile of walnuts and there are always some peanuts left over at the end of the day.

1. Based on Agustus' test, what are the results in terms of what nut the squirrels prefer?

   A. The squirrels do not like nuts

   B. The squirrels like both kinds of nuts the same

   C. The squirrels prefer walnuts

   D. The squirrels prefer peanuts

The Best Cold Medicine

Two scientists believe they have developed the best medicine for a cold. They ask 20 people to take the medicine when they come down with a cold. Medicine A seems to help people get better in about 2 weeks. Medicine B seems to help people get better in about 3 weeks.

2. Which medicine seems to help cure a cold better and why?

....

....

....

....

....

....

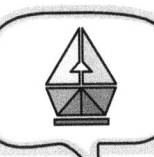
A Smarter Car

An engineer has decided to improve an electric car by making it more energy-efficient. He knows he can either make the car lighter in weight or put a different battery in it.

3. How could the engineer test which solution is better for making the electric car more efficient?

....

....

....

....

....

....

....

....

....

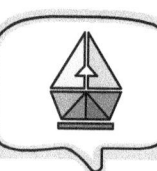
Yesterday, you explored how to test different solutions. Today you will explain how the results of these tests can help you determine which solutions are best.

Directions: Read each text below. Then answer the questions that follow.

Favorite Nuts

You discovered that squirrels prefer walnuts over peanuts based on Agustus' test.

1. If Agustus chose to fill all of the squirrel feeders in his neighborhood with peanuts, would he be choosing the best solution? Why or why not?

The Best Cold Medicine

You discovered that medicine A seems to cure a cold faster than medicine B.

2. How many people were tested?

3. Do you think it would be a good idea to test even more people?

    A. Yes

    B. No

A Smarter Car

You discovered that an engineer could test changes to an electric car design by making one version of the car that weighs less and one version of the car that has a better battery.

4. If the car that weighed less improved energy-efficiency better than the battery, which solution should the engineer choose as the best one?

....

....

....

....

....

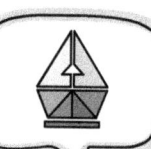

You have spent a few days looking at how the results from tests are used to determine the best solutions to design problems. Today you will analyze the results from a test done on a new type of snack.

Background:

Dimitri has created a new type of snack that tastes great and keeps you feeling full for up to ten hours! He wants to make sure he is not the only one who feels this way, however, and invites 7 of his friends to try it. He records results from the test which you can read in the table below.

Results To Dimiti's Test On His Snack Food:

Friend	Did They Like The Flavor Of Snack?	Did They Like The Texture Of Snack?	How Long Were They Full For After Eating The Snack?	Would They Eat This Snack Again
#1	Yes	Yes	5 hours	Yes
#2	No	No	4 hour	No
#3	Yes	No	6 hours	No
#4	Yes	No	10 hours	Yes
#5	Yes	No	5 hours	Yes
#6	No	Yes	5 hours	Yes
#7	Yes	No	6 hours	Yes

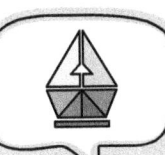
Follow-Up Questions:

1. Which friend did not like the texture or the taste of the snack?

....

....

2. Which friend was full for the longest after they ate the snack?

....

....

3. How many people would eat the snack again?

....

....

4. Do more people like or dislike the texture of the snack?

....

....

5. Did anyone like <u>both</u> the taste and the texture of the snack?

....

....

Yesterday, you analyzed the results from Dimitri's test on his snack food. Today you will elaborate on those findings and help Dimitri think about what design problems his snack has and what solution there might be to those problems.

Directions: Read and answer each question below.

1. Does this snack seem to keep people full for up to ten hours like Dimitri claims?

2. What seems to be the biggest design problem with his snack?

    A. The taste

    B. The texture

    C. If people would eat it again

3. What might be a solution to fix the texture of the snack?

4. Do you think Dimitri should ask more than 7 people?

5. Do you see how testing and results can help you pick the best solution to a design problem?

    A. Yes

    B. No

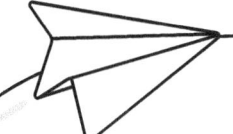

WEEK 20

Engineering

Improving Ideas & Designs

3-5-ETS1-3

Plan and carry out fair tests in which variables are controlled and failure points are considered to identify aspects of a model or prototype that can be improved.

ARGOPREP

Directions: Read the text below. Then answer the questions that follow.

Editing Your Ideas

When engineers and scientists come up with solutions to design problems, you've learned that they test their ideas and base their decisions off of results. Today you are going to explore how to improve ideas and designs through the process of **editing**. Editing is a very important part of the process and allows someone the ability to change their ideas in order to make them better. You may have heard about editing when it comes to writing - once you write a book, for example, it is important to read through what you wrote to make sure it makes sense and that everything is spelled correctly. Editing helps make something more accurate and therefore a better final product. The best thing about editing is that you can do it as many times as you like and each time you do it, you make your design better and better!

1. What is editing?

    A. Identifying a design problem

    B. Testing an idea

    C. Looking at results

    D. Changing your ideas and making them better

2. If you were going to edit a book, what changes might you make?

    A. Read the book

    B. Throw the book away

    C. Look for spelling mistakes

    D. Write a different book

3. How many times can you edit the design of something?

    A. Only once

    B. Once or twice

    C. As many times as you want

    D. I am not sure

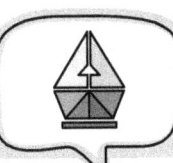
Yesterday, you learned that editing a design helps to improve it and that you can edit something more than once. Today you will explore the idea of editing with some activities.

Directions: Read each text below and complete the activity. Then answer the questions that follow.

Editing Writing

Read the following few sentences below and then rewrite them in the space below, editing any mistakes you notice. There are three mistakes total.

1. A robin was on the tRee in front of my window. It had a worm in itss beak that it was going to feed to the baby robins in its nest. I counted that there were for babies in the nest.

_____

_____

_____

_____

The Perfect Glasses

Pretend you designed a pair of glasses that are your favorite color and don't slip off your nose when you wear them. Your old pair of glasses always used to slip off of your nose so you decided to make a pair that did not have this design problem.. One day you notice that the glasses do fall off more frequently when you are exercising and sweating a lot.

2. Do you think the new design of your glasses are perfect? Why or why not?

_____

_____

_____

_____

Sweet Smells

Maggie has designed a new perfume that smells beautiful. Every single person she tested the perfume on said they loved the smell. One day someone who bought her perfume tells Maggie that the perfume smells great but the smell only lasts for about an hour.

3. What new design problem does Maggie have with her perfume?

....

....

....

4. Do you think Maggie needs to change the scent (the smell) of her perfume?

....

....

....

....

Yesterday, you explored how the editing process can help make designs even better. Today you will explain in more detail how the process of editing works.

Directions: Read each text below. Then answer the questions that follow.

Editing Writing

You discovered that editing your writing can help you improve it by getting rid of spelling and grammar mistakes.

1. Why is it a good idea to make sure your writing is spelled correctly and that it has good grammar?

....

....

....

The Perfect Glasses

You discovered that even though your new glasses fit better and don't slip off as much as the old design, they still slip off of your nose when you are sweating a lot.

2. Do you need to change the color of your glasses? Why or why not?

....

....

....

3. Do you see how changing the design again could make the glasses even better?

   A. Yes

   B. No

Sweet Smells

You discovered that even though everyone loves the smell of Maggie's perfume, the smell only lasts for about an hour.

4. Once Maggie edits the design of her perfume to make sure the scent lasts longer, should she test it again?

   A. Yes

   B. No

You have spent a few days Learning about how important the process of editing a design is. Today you will put these ideas to the test by experimenting with different designs for paper airplanes.

Materials:

1. Computer with internet
2. Paper
3. Ruler
4. Measuring tape

Procedure:

1. Go online and research different designs for paper airplanes. Look into designs that are pretty simple so that you feel like you can copy one easily.

2. Fold your paper into a paper airplane.

3. Take your paper airplane outside and mark a place on the ground where you will stand when you throw it.

4. Throw the paper airplane and measure how far it travels. Write the distance in the table on the next page under "Starting Design".

Example:

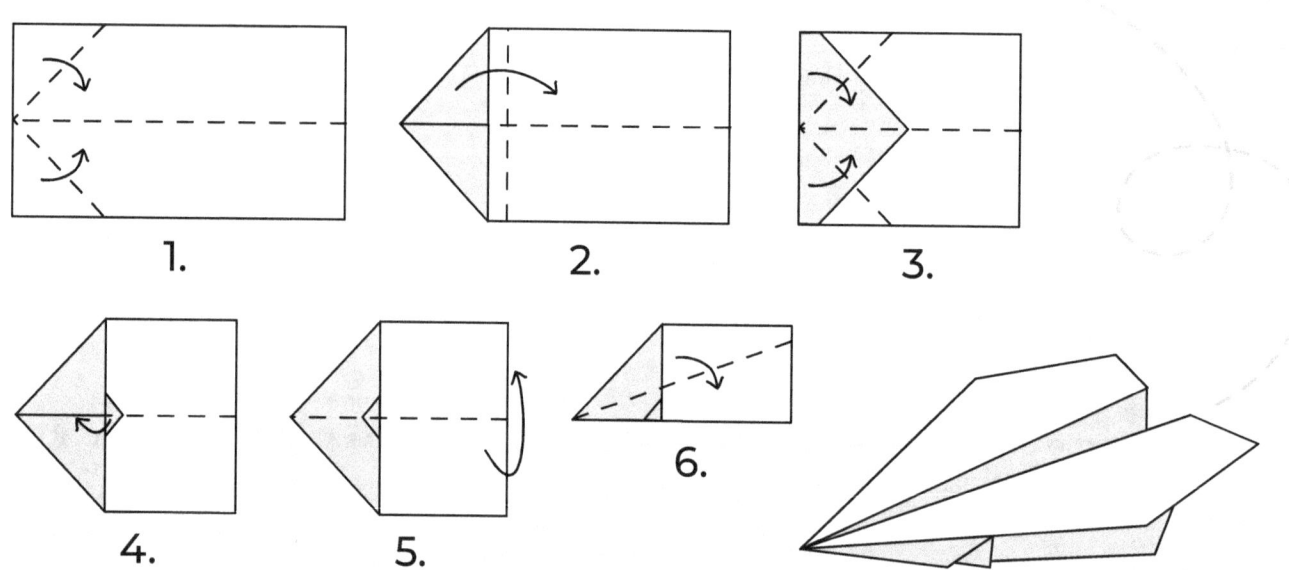

1.　　　　2.　　　　3.

4.　　　　5.　　　　6.

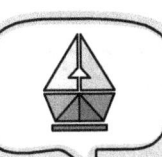
5. Now, try to change the design a little bit to see if you can make the paper airplane travel further. Maybe you make the wings shorter or you fold it into a different design you found on the internet.

6. Throw the second paper airplane design and record how far it traveled again. Write the distance in space under "Second Design".

7. Compete steps #5 and #6 a third time and then record the distance the final design travels under "Third Design" in the table.

Results Table:

	Starting Design	Second Design	Third Design
Distance Airplane Traveled			

Yesterday, you tested out a few designs for paper airplanes and changed your design a couple times through the process of editing. Today you will elaborate on this process and determine which edits you made to your design were the best ones.

Directions: Read and answer each question below.

1. Which paper airplane design worked the best?

2. Do you see how trying different designs helped to understand how different designs fly?

   A. Yes

   B. No

3. Do you think it would be helpful to try more designs to help you edit your design further?

   A. Yes

   B. No

4. Engineers edit their ideas to improve designs all the time! What is one thing you'd like to edit the design of?

5. Do you think the design of things can improve if people do not edit their work?

Answer Sheets

To see the answer key to the entire workbook, you can easily download the answer key from our website!

*Due to the high request from parents and teachers, we have removed the answer key from the workbook so you do not need to rip out the answer key while students work on the workbook.

 To watch free video explanations go to: **argoprep.com/science4** OR scan the QR Code:

Place your mouse over the workbook you have, and you will see the "Download Answers" button.

For detailed video instructions on how to access the "Answer Sheets," please scan this QR code.

6th Grade Science: Daily Practice Workbook | 20 Weeks of Fun

3rd Grade Science: Daily Practice Workbook | 20 Weeks of Fun...

4th Grade Science: Daily Practice Workbook | 20 Weeks of Fun...

7th Grade Science: Daily Practice Workbook | 20 Weeks of Fun...

5th Grade Science: Daily Practice Workbook | 20 Weeks of Fun...

8th Grade Science: Daily Practice Workbook | 20 Weeks of Fun...

Kindergarten Science: Daily Practice Workbook | 20 Weeks of Fun...

1st Grade Science: Daily Practice Workbook | 20 Weeks of Fun...

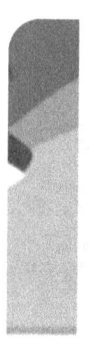

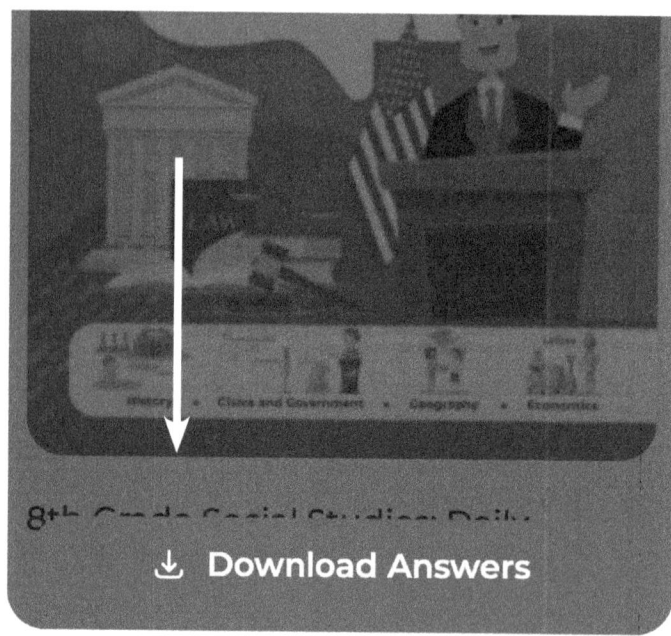

⬇ Download Answers

4th Grade Social Studies: Practice Workbook